Priceless

Priceless

TURNING ORDINARY PRODUCTS

INTO EXTRAORDINARY EXPERIENCES

Diana LaSalle

Terry A. Britton

HARVARD BUSINESS SCHOOL PRESS

Boston, Massachusetts

07 06 05 04 03   5 4 3 2 1

Requests for permission to use or reproduce material from this book should be directed to permissions@hbsp.harvard.edu, or mailed to Permissions, Harvard Business School Publishing, 60 Harvard Way, Boston, Massachusetts 02163.

Library of Congress Cataloging-in-Publication Data

LaSalle, Diana, 1949–
    Priceless : turning ordinary products into extraordinary experiences /
Diana LaSalle, Terry A. Britton.
        p. cm.
Includes index.
    ISBN 1-57851-746-X (alk. paper)
    1. Product management. 2. Design, Industrial. 3. Consumer behavior.
I. Britton, Terry. II. Title.
    HF5415.15 .L37 2002
    658.5'752—dc21

                                                    2002007421

The paper used in this publication meets the requirements of the American National Standard for Permanence of Paper for Publications and Documents in Libraries and Archives Z39.48-1992.

From Diana:

> To my son Aaron
> *for all that you are and all that you give.*
> *You are the most precious thread in my tapestry.*

From Terry:

> To my parents Lenard and Virginia,
> *who taught me all the important things in life.*
>
> And to my children, Kristina and Candice,
> *who showed me all the priceless things in life.*

Priceless:
of inestimable value

Contents

Beginnings xi
Special Thanks xvii

PART ONE
Value and Experience 1

one
My Kingdom for a Horse 5
The Key Is Value

two
When Is a Banana Not a Banana? 27
The Value Experience

three
The Journey Begins 47
The Experience Engagement Process

PART TWO

Creating Value through Experience 71

four
Getting a Grip 77
The Product Component

five
Was It Good for You, Too? 99
The Service Component

six
Surroundings 121
The Environment Component

seven
The Gift 145
From the Customer with Love

Notes 163
Index 173
About the Authors 181

Beginnings

It was only a matter of time before someone asked the big question: Why can't the MasterCard commercial be true and everything we buy lead to something priceless? Advertising promises it. Celebrity spokespersons allude to it. It's even safe to say that most businesses actually want to be a part of something priceless. But the fact remains that no matter how well intentioned a company might be, too often the ideal that "priceless" embodies is lost in the shuffle.

A case in point: One weekend Terry, a movie buff/technology junkie, purchased a state-of-the-art DVD player with six-speaker surround sound. Stopping at Hollywood Video on the way home, he carefully selected action-packed movies that would best show off his new toys. Three hours later, hookup and programming ritual complete, he tucked wires, boxes, and remotes neatly in place. After pouring a glass of wine, he dimmed the lights, reached for the translucent DVD case, and following a brief struggle to free it from its wrapper, he was ready—or so he thought.

Opening the case, Terry tried to remove the disc just as he would a music CD. Pushing on the plastic button protruding through the disc's center, he expected it to magically pop out. It didn't. Looking closer, he saw the instructions "lift here" near the disc's upper edge, so he did. Still nothing happened. Pulling on the flimsy disc, he attempted to balance pressure with concern over breaking it in two, but the DVD remained tightly in place. He was about to give up when his thumb came to rest on the center button while lifting the edge. Finally the disc popped free, but by now his earlier excitement was a thing of the past. The next morning, instead of remembering how great it was to see *The Matrix* in all its digital glory, he related how a poorly designed package tarnished his experience. Or in his words, "The last thing I needed at the end of the day was to feel too stupid to open a DVD."

We've all been there.

Whether it's a customer-proof package, a never-ending voice mail loop, a purchase that doesn't live up to its claims, or desired merchandise shelved two feet above the average person's head, we've all had expectations of product, performance, or service dashed by disappointment and frustration. Like most consumers, we've accepted these feelings as inevitable, but this time it struck home. Why *does* it have to be this way? With all the sophisticated technology, advanced study, and decades of know-how under our collective business belts, why are consumers continually disappointed and companies unable to please them?

Over the next few months we searched for the answer. We paid more attention to what we bought and used in our lives and how we felt, not just about a product but about everything surrounding it as well. How was it packaged? Was it accessible in stores? Did it deliver as promised? We even examined how people instinctively tried to use a product and whether their instincts ran contrary to the manufacturer's instructions. Often they did. Services were not ignored either. We noted how easy (or hard) it was to make an appointment and whether customer service representatives could actually solve customer problems.

In time, our curiosity and questioning became more of a quest, and we talked to others. Setting up consumer groups, we chronicled their stories and before long, two patterns emerged: First, when people reported their consumption experiences, good or bad, it wasn't just the product or service itself that created the reaction. Other factors such as the packaging on the DVD, an operating manual, a call center, or the ease of finding a product were also cited as contributing to the overall experience. Second, when people talked about an offering in terms of the experiences they had with it, they rarely confined their remarks to how well it did or didn't work. Their reports often included phrases like "It made me feel . . .", "It reminded me of . . .", or "It helped me to . . .".

These patterns ran contrary to traditional business, research, and marketing strategies, which focus first and foremost on features and benefits, but they fully supported the more innovative thinking of the time. For instance, in the *Journal of Consumer Research* article "The Experiential Aspects of Consumption: Consumer Fantasies, Feelings, and Fun," consumer research scholars Morris Holbrook and Elizabeth Hirschman noted the importance of looking at consumption from an "experiential view."[1] This perspective sees consumption as a subjective state with consumer behavior rooted more in the consumption experience than a snapshot decision based on feature and benefit analysis. In other words, instead of looking at consumers as logical thinkers who make purchasing decisions to solve problems—someone needs to open a can so she buys a can opener—they concluded it was more valid to look beyond the product to how it impacts consumers' lives.

This concept of viewing consumption as an experience rather than a singular event or decision was further explored in *The Experience Economy* by Joseph Pine II and James Gilmore. Widely credited with bringing experience to the forefront of business marketing, the authors make a convincing case that what people are looking for today are experiences (defined by them as "events that engage individuals in a personal way").[2] Furthermore, they show that in today's market, providing memorable experiences is good business. By charting the progression of economic value from goods to services and finally to experience, they demonstrate that the value of an offering that includes experience factors such as fun or entertainment is significantly higher than those lacking such attributes.[3] Our own research concurred.

When we examined companies most often noted as leaders in their industries, almost without exception they had one point in common—a mastery of enabling extraordinary experiences for their customers. These companies understood that for millions of people, owning a Harley isn't about owning a motorcycle—it's about breaking away from the confines of everyday life for a while. The iMac isn't about computing; it's about exploring virtual frontiers with ease. A professionally prepared tax return isn't about complying with government regulations; it's about peace of mind. Instead of mere products or services, consumers are buying freedom, adventure, and well-being. These are the intangible aspects of an offering that can't be measured, quantified, or reduced to features and benefits. They can only be experienced, and that ultimately is the value that can lead to something extraordinary—even priceless.

We began by wondering why the MasterCard commercial couldn't be true, and everything we buy with it lead to something priceless. The conclusion we reached is that often it can, and *Priceless* was written to show the way. We organized the book in two sections. The first is devoted entirely to understanding customers, value, and experience. The second part focuses on how businesses can deliver value through experience. Throughout the book, business stories and examples illustrate key concepts. The "Priceless Roadmap" at the end of chapters 1–6 recaps the key steps to help your company move toward an experience culture.

Those of you who have read Holbrook and Hirschman, Pine and Gilmore, Schmitt, and other early embracers of experience will find yourselves on familiar ground, for their work has certainly served as a foundation for our own.[4] *Priceless* builds on this foundation by (1) examining the relationship between value and experience and showing how linking the two can lead to greater customer satisfaction and loyalty, a more secure competitive position, and higher profits; (2) outlining the events a customer experiences during the consumption process, thus allowing a business to evaluate its own offerings for experience value; and (3) clearly showing how a company can deliver value through experience by focusing on three key components—product, service, and environment. In the end, we'll see how the customer himself can play a significant role in guiding product development, innovation, and delivery, ultimately becoming your partner and cocreator of a priceless experience. When this happens, your customers are happy, your company thrives, and your competition is left standing at the door.

Sound impossible? It's not.

History shows that any business, whether in manufacturing, service, or retail, that provides what the customer truly values can achieve real growth—not the growth of the past decade that has been eked out by downsizing, cost-cutting efficiencies, or megamergers, but the real thing. This growth—which according to a Deloitte & Touche study is *double* that of companies that do not put the customer first—is fed by value and measured in expanding market share and new, more-loyal customers.[5] It can be done. It *is* being done, as the companies featured in *Priceless* will show. They are perhaps the best proof that delivering value through experience works in the real world. If it can work for them, it can work for you.

If you are a decision maker responsible for business strategy, marketing, production, or delivery of goods or services, we believe you'll learn something from this book that will benefit your business and your customers. But our greatest hope is that what you learn in these pages will help your company move from one that sells ordinary goods and services toward one that delivers extraordinary experiences. Be warned, though. Once you read *Priceless*, you'll never look at what you sell—or buy—in the same way again.

Special Thanks

Writing this book has been an experience made more valuable by the help and encouragement of many people. Carol Alm, Darlene Caplan, Ric Deterding, Kellie Hale, Beckie Price, Aaron Sanders, Jenifer Sanders, Jerry Sanders, and Larry Shalzi—friends, colleagues, and smart people who shared ideas and questions with us. Clients and business associates who understood our distraction for almost a year and cut us some slack, especially Don Swanson. We promise to make it up to you. Our agent, John Willig, and our editors, Jacqueline Murphy and Genoveva Llosa, whose thoughtful probing brought out the best in *Priceless*. Your voices will always be with us. Finally, to our families—nothing we do in life is of any value without you to share it with.

PART ONE

Value and Experience

It was our custom during the writing of *Priceless* to venture out on shopping excursions in search of extraordinary products and services. Often we explored together, but on some occasions we'd go to a mall or concentrated area of stores, split up, and then rendezvous to compare notes. On this day, however, something unusual happened. Rushing into the coffee shop we'd set as our meeting place, Terry pulled up a chair and placed a package on the table.

"Wait until you see this," he said. "This is so cool."

Opening the package, he pulled out a hat—but not just any hat. This was a $62 *traveler's* hat and Terry didn't buy it for research, he bought it for himself. On the surface this might not seem strange, but you have to know Terry. To begin with, he is a city dweller who spends most of his time working, and never actually wears hats. True, the hat is good looking, at least by traveling-hat standards, and it won't sink (especially valuable in the Midwest). But still, he doesn't journey, hike, or trek. So even though he knows his $62 purchase will probably sit unused forever, he bought it anyway. The question was why? The answer, we discovered, was that he wasn't buying a hat after all. He was buying adventure.

From the moment Terry saw the Tilley hat, he was intrigued. The stylish head gear was carefully displayed to show off its best features, and signage proclaimed that it ties on in the wind, it won't shrink, it's a sun hat, it's a rain hat, and it floats. The company also boldly stated that its product is acknowledged best in the world and insured against loss! Surely this begged further investigation. Taking up the Owner's Manual included with every hat, Terry read about sailing sloops and America's Cup races. One happy archaeologist proclaimed he "crossed the Sahara in an unsinkable [Tilley] hat," while another reported that "I was robbed of my . . . Tilley Hat at gunpoint . . . I must say that other than fearing for my life, I was extremely upset in losing my new hat. . . . Please send me a new 7 5/8 ASAP." With a little nudge of the imagination, Terry could see himself joining the ranks of Tilley owners such as these, sailing the seas, exploring ancient artifacts in some exotic country, or warding off rogues in dark alleys.

If he were to purchase a Tilley hat, Terry would also receive Tilley Brag Tags, which read

> *Most Tilley Hat wearers, and the person beside you is a prime ex-ample, are interesting people of sterling character. It's well worth cultivating their acquaintance! To that end, you'll be pleased to learn, it is customary to provide the giver of Tilley Hat procure-ment information (such as this card) with a warm hug, or stand him or her to a drink.*

Terry couldn't resist. Adventure, fun, social interaction—the Tilley was no longer a simple chapeau. It was an object that stirred his over-worked soul and helped him see life through new eyes, if only for a while. Sixty-two dollars really was a small price to pay for such a feeling—for such an *experience*.

Consumer experts have been telling us for years that what people want is experience and that the only way to succeed is to deliver just such a feeling. Unfortunately for most companies, it's easier said than done. To begin with, in order to deliver experiences, we have to under-stand why people want experiences. Why is a person like Terry attracted to a traveling hat? True, it promised him adventure, but was that, by itself, enough to make him part with $62 for something he didn't need? We'll find out as we explore people's motivations to buy in chapter 1. This exploration uncovers the very nature of consumer value and how people recognize or experience value. We'll also look at how value has evolved over time and show that, today people expect value delivered through experiences.

Armed with this insight, our next task will be to answer some questions: What *is* an experience? Does it happen in an instance or last a lifetime? Is it a singular event or a series of happenings? Chapter 2 addresses these questions and then shows how value and experience come together to deliver the ultimate prize—the Value Experience. During this discussion, we'll introduce rewards and sacrifices—the ultimate measure of overall value. If a product delivers significantly more rewards than sacrifices, it leads to a Value Experience. Too many sacrifices, and you have a product customers will avoid the second time around.

Finally, in order to allow you to see your products through the critical eyes of the consumer, chapter 3 takes you step-by-step through the Experience Engagement Process. This is a five-stage process that begins with the urge to buy and progresses until a product is integrated into a person's life or, if you're lucky, extended into a relationship beyond the offering itself. It's an interesting journey, one that most companies have never made, and it can be a real eye-opener. But before we begin our voyage, we have to see a man about a horse.

CHAPTER **one**

My Kingdom for a Horse

THE KEY IS VALUE

A horse! a horse! my kingdom for a horse!
—WILLIAM SHAKESPEARE, *KING RICHARD III*, ACT 5, SCENE 4.

I N FIFTEENTH-CENTURY ENGLAND, HANGING ON to the royal crown was a constant struggle. Enemies were everywhere, but for King Richard III none was more formidable than the Earl of Richmond. As we join the king, we find him engaged in heated battle with the army of his foe. Amid clashing swords and clanging armor, the king and his men fight valiantly, but one by one they fall. Finally the king's own horse is slain, and his fate is clear. Powerless to retreat, he turns to face death and in an anguished voice he cries . . . well, you get the picture.

While it's doubtful Shakespeare intended it at the time, the words he put in his doomed king's mouth were the perfect example of how value works in the marketplace. When something has enough value, a person will pay anything to have it. On the other hand, without value there's not much reason to buy. It's doubtful King Richard would have given his kingdom for a horse if he were standing in the middle of the Royal Stables. Faced with certain destruction, however, nothing was worth more than a swift steed—not even his crown.

As consumers ourselves, we can understand his feelings. At one time or another we've all made purchases that made us feel good, look good, or, like the king, helped solve a pressing problem. In other words, we made purchases based on the value the purchase provided. This is the nature of value. It motivates us to buy and determines what we are willing to pay. In fact, value is the basis for all consumption.[1]

In this chapter we'll define value and explore how people sense it on various levels—physical, emotional, intellectual, and spiritual. We'll also look at *Value Groups,* or collections of individuals who share and sense value in similar ways. Here and there we'll stop to meet companies that increased sales, produced higher margins, and created customer loyalty through the use of value concepts. Their stories will help us understand not only the workings of value but also why everyone in business should strive to master them. Keep in mind that even though you may not recognize your exact business situation in examples and stories, each offers a way of thinking that can be applied to any product or service. Part of what we hope you gain from reading *Priceless* is a different way of looking at your offerings and the place they hold in your customers' lives. These examples will help. But first things first—what exactly is value?

The Nature of Value

VALUE AS IT RELATES to consumption has fascinated scholars for decades. In fact, there is a field of study called *axiology* that has produced volumes of thinking by recognized authorities who delved into the social, psychological, economic, and even spiritual foundations of value.[2] What they determined is that while value is based on a variety of criteria, it boils down to one simple fact—the final value of an offering is determined by the consumer. *Value is in the eye of the beholder.* This is the key to unlocking the mystery of value.

Only the buyer can determine what value he or she finds in a purchase. Only an individual can determine what that value is worth in terms of payment. So if this is the case, how can we understand or ultimately predict what people will value?

To begin with, we need to understand the criteria people use to assign value. These criteria are both objective and subjective. The first relates to the essential nature of a product or the offering's inherent value. A gold ring, for example, has inherent material value based on its weight and carat. This is easy to understand because weight and carat are tangible and measurable. On the other hand, subjective criteria are based on the symbolic or associative value of a product.[3] In the case of the ring, the criteria might include the beauty of the design, the reputation of the jeweler, or what the ring represents. A class ring might symbolize loyalty and camaraderie; an engagement ring, love and the promise of marriage. All products and services possess some elements of objective and subjective criteria, and both contribute to the overall value of an offering. They also help determine what the consumer considers a fair and reasonable price. As we examine each, we'll refer to them as *objective value* and *subjective value* rather than criteria. Keep in mind, however, that they are not really different types of value but different means of *determining* value. Let's look at the objective variety first.

Objective value is based on criteria such as availability, size, quantity, hours to manufacture, and so on. For example, when OPEC opens up oil production, gasoline is more available and therefore less expensive to purchase. When they tighten production, lessening the supply, fuel becomes more valuable. We can measure availability, so it's easy to justify paying more or less. The same is true for other types of objective criteria. A large bottle of soda delivers more product than a small one; therefore we have no problem accepting that it costs more. An automobile takes more materials and time to manufacture than a bicycle, so we expect to pay more for a Chevy than a Schwinn.

Efficiency and cost savings also qualify as objective value because they are quantifiable. The Industrial Containers Division of Sonoco

Product Company, which produces fiber and plastic drums, conducts what it calls "cost-in-use studies" to document the incremental cost savings their products bring to customers. Working with the customer they perform a series of process-flow analyses that outline the company's entire business operations and estimate their costs. Using these estimates, the Sonoco team can suggest solutions, such as a complete materials-handling system, to improve efficiency and save the customer money.[4] Because the savings are based on the customer's actual environment, Sonoco is able to offer significant objective value to its customers that is both measurable and tangible. The persuasive power of quantifiable value based on fact is one reason why businesses often turn to this type of value to attract and retain customers.

Subjective value, on the other hand, is much more elusive. Where objective value is tangible and measurable, subjective value is just the opposite. According to Marsha L. Richins, professor of marketing at the University of Missouri, Columbia, and a recognized expert on materialism, "It is not the goods themselves that people desire, but rather the benefits these goods provide—an increase in comfort or pleasure, the ability to accomplish new tasks, the esteem of others when they regard what we own."[5] This is subjective value. It is what a product or service means to an individual as a result of the benefits derived from using and owning it.

For example, a woman has a cell phone that she uses to keep in close contact with her children while family members go about their day. They call her to let her know where they are or if they need something. She feels this phone helps her be a better mom, so it has a very emotional and personal meaning for her and therefore great value. That's why she spends the extra money each month to have a cell phone as well as her normal telephone at home. Another person might buy a book to learn a new skill that helps her on the job. The subjective value she receives from her book is very different, but no less important than the value the mom with the cell phone receives. They just experience their value in different ways—the mom on an emotional level and the book reader on a more intellectual plane. As consumers we perceive or recognize value, especially subjective value, in different ways and on different levels.

Value and the Whole Person

P SYCHOLOGISTS have suggested that as human beings we oper-
ate on four levels: physical, emotional, intellectual, and spiritual.[6]
On the physical plane, we deal with basic survival needs as well as sensations such as comfort and pleasure. Experienced through the senses,
the physical level is the one on which all goods and services are perceived, because all offerings have some sensory element attached to them.
If a product or service can be seen, heard, tasted, touched, or smelled, it
will register on the physical level.

The intellectual level is where people process learning and skills,
evaluate preferences, appreciate excellence, and strive for mastery. If
a thought process is engaged in any way, the intellectual level is involved. For instance, it is your intellect that is often the first to recognize
objective value since it is the mind that calculates savings, processes
the concept of supply and demand, and so on. The intellect also registers satisfaction when a product works as promised or has to decide
what to do when it doesn't. When Terry couldn't get the DVD out of its
case, initially at least, this affected him on the intellectual level. After a
few minutes, frustration moved the product onto the next level.

By its very nature, the emotional level is the hardest to predict and
control. Personal and changeable, it is very much a part of subjective
value. Through our emotions we are able to recognize and share love,
nurture others and ourselves, and feel friendship. This is also the level
where loyalty is fostered. Our reason or intellect might tell us that, logi-
cally, we should continue doing business with a company that takes good
care of us, but it is our emotional being that feels compelled to do so. On
the other hand, people also feel anger, frustration, and annoyance, so the
opposite of loyalty—rapid desertion—also begins in this fragile space.

The final level is the spiritual realm. Generally thought of as a reli-
gious connection, we define it to mean anything that touches our core
being. Beauty, art, creativity, and self-awareness all reside at this complex
level. And while many of the values we identify as being on the spiritual
level also engage the other levels of consciousness—art, for example,

engages our senses as well as our minds and emotions—they have an unexplainable quality that can only be described as touching our soul or awakening something deep within. If you've ever walked on a beach and felt instantly at peace, this is the spiritual level of your being at work.

Experiencing life on these four levels makes life richer and helps us to be complete human beings, or what behavioral sciences often refer to as the *whole person*. More important for our discussion, however, is the fact that these various levels also help us determine the value of what we purchase—and what we sell. What or how great that value is depends largely on how a product or service affects the various levels. Let's apply this theory to a product and see how it works. For simplicity's sake, we'll start with a candle.

Seeing Value in a New Light

On one of our shopping trips, we found a plain white candle at a hardware store. The merchandising and packaging made it clear the candle was intended for use as a backup in case of a power outage at home or a flashlight failure at camp—in other words, it provides light when other sources fail. Light allows us to see, so we know the candle makes contact with us on the physical level. Later, however, we were in another store and saw a similar candle. This one was also made of white wax, but it was scented as well. This added a new dimension to the product. Now the candle wasn't just a source of light; it also produced an enjoyable fragrance. This changed the impact of the candle and therefore its value.

We have a friend whose master bath has an inviting recessed tub set in a garden window. The window is filled with flowers and nearly a dozen scented white candles like the ones we saw on our shopping trip. Several times a week she soaks away the tensions of the day surrounded by the glow of candlelight and the smell of gardenias. Like the first candle, these are made of wax and provide illumination. However, they also provide a sense of comfort and self-nurturing, encourage relaxation, and create a beautiful environment. Because these candles affect her on multiple levels, in this case the physical, emotional, and spiritual levels, they not only have different value, they have more value.

Think back to our description of objective value. One of the criteria was quantity—the more volume a product or service offers, the more value it is perceived to deliver. The same principle works here. The more impact a product has on the levels of consciousness, the more value it has. A candle that not only provides light (objective value) but adds comfort and self-nurturing (subjective value) as well is perceived to be worth more than one that provides only light. Since it is perceived to be worth more, businesses can charge more. The first candle, whose intended use was solely to provide light, can be purchased for $2. The second candle, manufactured and marketed to appeal to the emotional and spiritual levels, can cost $8 or more. That's a 400 percent increase in price based on the heightened impact the product provides. It's also interesting to note that while most people have only two or three "backup" candles in their home for emergencies, our friend has more than twenty "comfort" candles. *Greater impact, greater value, greater sales.* Or as the MasterCard commercial might put it—

Matches	*10 cents*
Candle	*$8*
Relaxation	*Priceless*

Just as the candle can be presented as an ordinary source of light or a priceless source of comfort and relaxation, many of your products can also be redefined in terms of the value they offer. All it takes is a different view of what you're selling and a different way to determine value.

The Value Model

EARLIER WE TALKED about the fact that most companies determine pricing based on objective value such as cost to produce, market, distribute, and sell as well as criteria such as supply and demand. We've also learned that by adding subjective value to the equation, we can often increase the worth of a product. To do this, however, you first need to identify what consumers really want from your products and what additional impact you might offer to increase their value.

To facilitate identification, we constructed a model that lists the primary qualities valued by consumers in the products and services they purchase, grouped by the ways in which they are perceived—on the physical, emotional, intellectual, or spiritual level (see table 1-1). The attributes listed on the model were compiled from the works of noted experts in psychology, human sciences, and axiology such as Abraham Maslow, Mihaly Csikszentmihalyi, Morris Holbrook, Marsha L. Richins, and Bernd H. Schmitt.[7] As you examine and work with the model, you may discover that your product or service offers a unique value that is not represented on this model. That's fine. Just add it to the appropriate level. What's important is to begin to recognize the value your offering represents. The easiest way to do this is to *change your perspective from what a product or service is or what it does to what it offers*. For instance, a potato peeler isn't just a kitchen tool, it's a convenience. Neon-colored Post-it Notes aren't just office supplies, they're efficiency with a little enjoyment thrown in. The Pentium III isn't just a microchip, it's a high-performance pathway to the digital world wrapped in a reputation for quality and excellence. It's all a matter of perspective.

Once you've begun to see your products and services in terms of the types of value they provide, think about what else they could offer if you made a few adjustments. That first white candle, for instance, was plain, simple, and provided light. Adding scent expanded the impact of the candle on the senses and, with the help of product displays and marketing, associated the candle with relaxation, comfort, and nurturing, thus increasing its value. We view this as *cumulative value*, a phenomenon that happens when a product registers multiple hits on one or more levels of consciousness.

The Pentium chip is another good example. It scores three hits on the intellectual level—performance, quality, and a reputation for excellence. This makes it more valuable than a product that may have the same performance and quality but doesn't have an established reputation for excellence, as in the case of AMD, a Pentium chip rival.[8] They

TABLE 1 - 1

Value Model

Physical	Emotional	Intellectual	Spiritual
Exhilaration	Well-being	Learning	Fulfillment
Pleasure	Personal growth	Knowledge	Peace
Comfort	Recognition	Appreciation	Freedom
Convenience	Nurturing	Rarity	Trust
Independence	Caring	Excellence	Integrity
Security	Relationships	Control	Spiritual growth
Survival	Status	Quality	Spiritual expression
	Self-expression	Choice	Creative expression
	Self-esteem	Reliability	Aesthetic connection
	Belonging	Consistency	Social conscience
	Happiness	Satisfaction	
	Harmony	Performance	
	Personal identity	Efficiency	

offer a fine product, but because chip performance is so critical to computing, Intel's reputation provides more intellectual impact and therefore more value in the mind of the consumer.

As human beings, we all need shelter. That basic need certainly falls in the physical level—a roof over our heads is necessary for survival against the elements. But if that roof is also in a safe neighborhood, it adds security. Make it bigger and fancier, and comfort and enjoyment come into the mix along with the possible inclusion of status and satisfaction. Everyone would agree this house offers more value than the first. Put a cottage on a lake, ocean, or in the mountains, however, and it makes its way to aesthetic connection, maybe even peace. Now we're talking serious value. By impacting the consumer on multiple levels, you've gone from a basic need to a riot of worth that touches the entire being. In this context it makes sense that so many people want to retire to the beach and are willing to pay significantly more for the privilege.

Most of us can intuitively accept this concept of cumulative value as true. In fact, we can all cite examples of how it has worked in our own lives. The real test, however, is how it works on a larger scale. Because the candle has been so helpful in illustrating our points, it seems appropriate to look at one company whose products bring multiple levels of value to millions of people each year. The company is Illuminations, the nation's leading specialty retailer of candles and home décor accessories.

Illuminations

Launched in 1996 with four stores in Chicago, Boulder, and Santa Clara and Corte Madera, California, Illuminations is the brainchild of entrepreneur Wally Arnold.[9] Arnold's company fascinates us not just for the fact that it has proven to be very successful in its short existence—in 2001 Illuminations had seventy-five stores with sales of $100 million—but because it was able to succeed by convincing consumers to make candles a part of everyday living.[10] From the beginning, the company was founded on a value-based vision—"to inspire you to live every day by candlelight"—or in essence to take time out of a fast-paced, stressful life to relax, nurture yourself, bring beauty to your surroundings, and even have a little fun.[11] This vision is evident in everything the company does, from the atmosphere in their stores to the products they carry and the way employees are trained to interact with customers.

When you walk into an Illuminations store, you are immediately immersed in a relaxing and inspiring environment. Walls of candles arranged by color and scent make sampling the different aromas easy and inviting. We've seen people spend half an hour just smelling candles. Displays throughout the store featuring centerpieces and arrangements also help customers discover different ways to use candles in their homes. We especially like the fact that all the components of an arrangement on display are grouped together near the display. Containers, candleholders, candles, and even seasonal decorations are all at the customer's fingertips. This makes it convenient to gather and buy what one needs to re-create an arrangement at home. If a customer wants a unique candle arrangement, employees are on hand to suggest color, shape, and fragrance combinations.

For those who wish to shop from home, Illuminations has a mail-order catalog and Web site. The photography for both is so inviting it makes you want to order just to capture the same glow for your own home. The Web site also serves an educational purpose. It has use and safety tips, candle folklore, decorating ideas, and a self-care section with relaxation suggestions. All of these extra touches in the store, catalog, and Web site help drive home the value Illuminations's products bring to the customer. What's more, not only is the company focused on delivering the value of candlelight to everyday living, it doesn't leave it up to the customer to discover that value. Through its marketing and merchandising, it makes sure everyone knows its products offer relaxation, comfort, nurturing, romance, and beauty.

The benefit of broadcasting this value up front is twofold. First, the customer can quickly determine what the product is worth to her—remember, value is personal—and second, when the customer picks up a product and sees a premium price, she's not surprised. Furthermore, she's willing to pay the price because she already knows the value she's receiving in exchange for her dollars. So the customer receives greater value and the company, higher margins. But that's not all value does for the company. Remember our friend with the twenty comfort candles? She bought all of them at Illuminations. In fact, she shops there regularly. When a business consistently delivers value, people come back. By focusing on value, Illuminations can command premium prices, sell more product, and foster customer loyalty. Any business can do the same, even if it has already fallen into the dreaded category of commodity.

Pumping out Value

Perhaps the greatest challenge any company faces today is commoditization—the process through which a product becomes so common place that differentiation becomes difficult and the lowest price rules.[12] The gasoline industry knows better than most how challenging commoditization can be. In this industry, price wars not only take place from company to company but often from corner to corner. So how can a commodity like gasoline offer value beyond basic needs? Let's visit a BP Connect location for a look at what one company spokesman rightly calls, "the gas station of the future."[13]

Even from the road, BP Connect announces it is different from the ordinary gas station.[14] Bright green and yellow signage combined with futuristic gas pumps and curved building contours are inviting and distinctive. At the fueling islands, the gas pump touch pads offer quick purchase options as expected, but these Internet-connected machines not only look advanced, they are. Everything from weather updates and road conditions to news headlines and travel directions can be accessed while you fuel.

"Think about it," says Robert Mead, president of Chicago-based SQAD, one of the companies BP worked with to design its point-of-purchase strategies. "You're at the pump putting gas in, and you look around, back and forth, up and down, and you're bored. But now, this screen is allowing you to interface with information. It's enticing you to do more . . . by looking up directions for your destination, or by checking the weather because you're traveling."[15]

The enticement doesn't stop at information, however. "One of the challenges with convenience stores that sell gasoline is getting the customer off the pump island and into the store to make a purchase," Mead says.[16] So the pumps offer the option to order food from the Wild Bean Café located just inside the store. With this handy feature, customers can place an order on the screen and their food will be waiting for them when they enter the store. The pumps also let customers know about in-store specials.

Once inside, patrons find an equally futuristic convenience store. "We're carrying the products people are looking for," says John Anderson, manager of U.S. marketing and merchandising for BP Amoco. "More variety in health and beauty aids, more variety in what's in our coolers."[17] Customers also told the company they like fresh food offerings, so the coffee-shop-style Wild Bean Café serves freshly made gourmet salads, custom sandwiches, soups, and fresh pastries along with coffee, cappuccino, tea, and fountain drinks. Internet connections inside allow the customer to stop for lunch and check out the traffic at the same time.

Since the stores are fairly new, it's too soon to tell if BP Connect will revolutionize the gas station/convenience store industry, but early indications are promising. One customer from Algonquin, Illinois, who was interviewed shortly after a new BP Connect opened in her area, was on her second visit to the store that week. "And I didn't even need gas today," she said.[18] Bringing in repeat customers for more than gasoline is key to the concept stores' success, and BP has given people many obvious reasons to do just that. To its credit, BP also offers customers another reason to support the new venture, this one not so obvious, but nonetheless compelling.

Outside each store, a translucent canopy located just above the gas pumps generates electricity from the sun. These solar devices gather enough energy to provide from 5 percent to 25 percent of the energy needed at a site, depending on its geographic location. BP officials conservatively estimate each store saves enough energy to fuel five or six homes a day. On the surface, this attention to the environment may not seem significant, but in terms of consumer value, it is. A Gallup poll found that 73 percent of the respondents bought a product specifically because they thought it was better for the environment than competing products.[19] So in addition to time savings, traveler support, convenience, and a pleasurable shopping and dining experience, customers can feel good about supporting an environmentally responsible fuel company. This list of value-laden offerings isn't something you would expect from a company that started out selling a commodity. But then the commodity—gasoline—is only a small part of what it offers, and therein lies the lesson.

When a product or service becomes a commodity, the only way to pull above the fray is to give customers additional value so that price is not the deciding factor, just as BP has done. It wrapped its commodity in efficiency and convenience and then expanded its offerings to include other products and services its customers can access at the same time. The company was so successful in this transformation from commodity to value offering that today it would be inaccurate to call BP

Connect a gas station or even a convenience store. In terms of value, it is much more. To the traveler, it's a source of information. To the pit-stopper, it's a time-saver. To "green shoppers," it's a partner in preserving the environment. In each case BP understood what the customer valued and delivered it with considerable style.

If value can be built into a commodity such as gasoline or a product as simple as a candle, it can be done with any product or service in any market. BP and Illuminations both demonstrate that if you recognize and listen to your customers' needs, add the objective and subjective value necessary to meet those needs, and then advertise this greater value, customers will come, they'll stay, and they'll pay a premium price to do business with you. The challenge is to recognize the value your customers will respond to.

The Herding Instinct

A S INDIVIDUAL as we believe we are, humans tend to group to-gether based on a variety of characteristics. The most obvious are nationality, race, and creed, but when it comes to consumption, there is another set of herding instincts. These are based on shared values, and when enough people share the same values and perceive them in the same way, you have a *Value Group*. BP, for instance, serves at least three different constituencies—travelers, local drivers, and environmentally aware shoppers. Each of these is a Value Group, and each group is look-ing for something different from its visit to BP Connect. So, how can you determine what your customers value so you can organize them into Value Groups?

For decades, businesses have relied on market research to identify marketing opportunities and give advanced warning of significant changes in consumer behavior. Traditionally, research has focused largely on de-mographic and psychographic data such as age, sex, location, social group, interests, frequency of use, and so forth.[20] This information tells com-panies what consumers look like and how they behave, but it doesn't tell them what people value in their purchases. Since all consumption is based on value, this is vital information. Without it you cannot define your value offering or communicate its merit to your customers.

Over the past two decades great strides have been made in research methodologies to identify what consumers value. One of the most interesting is referred to as *laddering*.[21] With this structured interview method, consumers are asked to identify what is important to them about a product, service, or a particular attribute. This often requires several layers of probing (thus the name laddering), but the eventual result is the uncovering of the personal value realized by the consumer. For example, if someone is asked why he uses whitening toothpaste, he might say to have whiter teeth. If probed further to find out why this is important to him, the consumer may say it makes him look better, a typical features/benefits type of response. When asked again, he may finally reveal that looking better gives him greater confidence and self-esteem. These, then, are the values the product represents, and the Value Group would be people who gain confidence and self-esteem through their appearance.

You can take the laddering approach a step further by using the Value Model to identify that this group of consumers recognizes these values on the emotional level. Once you identify and group your customers by the value they receive and how they recognize that value, you can craft more effective communications and uncover new opportunities to refine or expand the value of your offerings.

One of the exercises we did early on in our exploration of value was to ask people to identify their most prized possession and relate why it was important to them. One woman chose a serigraph that she proudly displays in her living room. A beautiful piece of art, its aesthetics are only a small part of the value she places on it. Its primary value lies in the fact that her husband bought it for her while they were on a long-awaited trip to Italy.

While wandering through Venice, the couple discovered a small gallery. After admiring one particular piece for several minutes, the dealer approached them and began talking about the serigraph's tone and mood and the artist's history. He closed with a rehearsed speech about its investment value, which would doubtless go up each year, and then graciously backed away, telling them to think about it. Within a few minutes the couple left, not having made a decision. Later in the afternoon, the wife mentioned again how beautiful the serigraph was and how it had captured the feeling of Venice for her. On the way back to their hotel, they revisited the gallery. Seeing them approach, the gallery owner smiled largely, welcoming them back with open arms.

"Ah, I knew you couldn't pass up such an investment," he said. "I can always tell. You will have no regrets."

They let him ramble on for a few minutes, but never once did he mention what a wonderful reminder of their trip this would be, and that's really why she wanted it. Fortunately for the gallery owner, her husband was more astute. Despite the fact that the acquisition was not in their vacation budget, he bought it for her anyway. Now every time his wife looks at the serigraph hanging in their home, she is reminded of their time together in Italy. By recognizing the true value of the artwork, the thoughtful husband transformed it from something bought to something cherished.

As for the dealer, he was probably quite proud of making the sale, but in reality he came very close to losing it unnecessarily. Because the gallery attracts many foreign tourists, its primary Value Group consists of people building memories. A secondary Value Group might be those interested in investment, but they would exhibit different characteristics, perhaps asking about appreciation of the artist's work, collectors, and so on. Identifying the characteristics and needs of your Value Groups and making sure your employees also recognize those traits can help you improve your sales numbers and leave customers feeling understood and cared for. In addition, when you understand your Value Groups, you are better able to respond when their needs change just as our next company did.

At the Ready

During the last decade of the twentieth century many companies in the fast-growing middle market segment were accustomed to growth driving healthy profit margins. Increased consumer demand and a booming business-to-business marketplace kept revenues high and everyone busy. At the turn of the millennium, however, all that changed. In 2001 the most remarkable period of sustained economic growth in modern U.S. history came to a screeching halt. With the economy rapidly shrinking, it became painfully clear that these midsized companies needed to find new ways to sustain profit margins.

Recognizing this need in its middle market Value Group, American Express was ready to help. "Our experience with tens of thousands of midsized companies was that there were almost always hidden pockets of wasted money that could be converted to margin improvement if you knew where to look," said Anre Williams, vice president and general manager of American Express Corporate Services Middle Market unit.[22] For example, at many of these companies, employees use petty cash or their own personal credit cards to purchase travel services, small office supplies, and computer equipment for remote offices. As a result, the companies had no real control over the volume and extent of purchases. Worse yet, firms spent huge amounts of time and money on cash advances and invoice-to-check processing. With an American Express Corporate Card program, however, companies could exercise better control over these discretionary spend categories, and money saved flowed directly to the bottom line. When the economy slowed, American Express took the initiative to market this value to its distressed Value Group. It was a case of being in the right place at the right time, and its customers benefited from the timing. Case in point: Wacker Chemical Corporation, a Michigan-based chemical company.[23]

For years, the company's senior management resisted accounting supervisor Sandy Lewis's suggestion that they use a corporate card for expenses. Instead it had been the company's policy to have employees use personal credit cards for travel and checks for remote office needs. Because of this rule, Lewis was constantly scrambling to issue emergency checks when employees hit their credit limits or didn't submit expense reports in time to meet their credit card deadlines. She also had to issue cash advances for relocation expenses and more expensive overseas trips, as well as track down issues like reimbursements for flights booked but later refunded.

When new management was charged with streamlining expenses, however, the American Express message finally got through and Lewis was given the green light to get things under control. First, she issued American Express Corporate Cards to all traveling employees. With no preset spending limit, the Corporate Card eliminated the need for cash advances even for more expensive foreign travel. Offsite salespeople working from virtual offices were also encouraged to put everyday office needs on the card. "These are generally retail purchases, and it's more convenient for these remote employees than using purchase orders," said Lewis. It was also easier to set up new employees with credit. With American Express's online services, she could issue cards immediately to new employees to cover relocation expenses, usually getting cards in their hands in less than forty-eight hours. As an added bonus, the Corporate Card solved the problem of establishing credit accounts for foreign nationals who had no U.S. credit history.

Lewis found that in addition to the convenience and efficiency the program brought her company, she was able to uncover some unexpected savings. Within a short time of establishing a relationship with American Express, Lewis became an active user of the online servicing center, American Express @ Work. This feature allows Corporate Card administrators to handle program management tasks in real time. Now Lewis could quickly identify accounts that were getting late and remind employees to stay current, or immediately cancel cards as employees left the company. The Web site also cut down on much of the busywork she used to do. Employees who were on the road and hadn't seen their card statements would frequently call Lewis and ask her to check their balances or look up transactions they needed to file on their expense reports. Now they could look it up themselves with American Express's online "Check Your Bill" service.

Saving this time allowed Lewis to monitor other expenses more closely. For example, she spotted an alarming trend in nonrefundable airline ticket-exchange fees, which added up quickly at $100 per charge. Once she identified the trend, she was able to institute changes to control expenses. Wacker Chemical's purchasing manager also used the data available on American Express @ Work to negotiate with vendors for discounts the company didn't know it was entitled to before the program. As for employees, Lewis says they are "thrilled to no longer be the company bank," keeping personal card accounts clear of corporate expenses.[24]

One of the reasons American Express was able to deliver the right value and value message at the right time is because it continually conducts research and solicits feedback from customers. Gathering this information is important not only to respond quickly to current issues, such as a weak economy, but also to spot trends of evolving values. Tracking value per se is not something companies have been accustomed to doing, but it should be, because major shifts in value can have a significant impact on their business.

Evolution

N EARLY ALL BUSINESSPEOPLE today would agree that understanding customers and giving them what they want is one of the greatest challenges to success. Part of the problem is that as a species, man continues to grow and change, building on past experiences and lessons learned. The same is true of the consumer—people evolve, and as they evolve what they value changes or, more accurately, it shifts. For example, when a person can sustain basic survival needs, he is able to change his focus from putting food on the table to having a more comfortable and entertaining life. It doesn't mean basic survival is no longer important; it just isn't a major focus because it is easily sustainable. Put another way, you might say that what was once extraordinary—having food on the table every day—is now ordinary.

Values also evolve through the changing or expansion of a person's definition of value. In pioneer days, housing comfort meant a roof over one's head. Today a house must have central heating and cooling to be considered comfortable. In the future, household comfort might mean zoned climate control such as the kind we see in luxury automobiles. Thus, values can evolve when something extraordinary becomes ordinary or when the definition of value changes or expands.

Every business goes through times when values evolve within its Value Groups in the ways we've just described. VCRs were once the rage, but once the market was saturated with them, the machine was no longer extraordinary, so its value decreased. In the early 1900s, women spent fifty-eight hours a week on household chores, so the value recognized as convenience in the first decades of the twentieth century was usually attached to home appliances that made housework easier.[25] Today the definition of convenience in the home has been expanded to include services such as housekeeping and home delivery of everything from food to computer repairs. We consider both of these to be cases of microevolution—or evolutionary stages within a specific category or industry, such as home entertainment or home convenience. This type of evolution is often fueled by technology and can change rapidly and often. It's important to understand what's happening to values at this level, especially when doing near-future planning. For example, once it became apparent that adoption of the VCR would be widespread, it was safe to assume that the extraordinary-to-ordinary rule would apply, and you could begin looking to the next extraordinary advancement in home entertainment such as the DVD.

In addition to these more targeted cycles, however, we must also be aware of the bigger picture. It is when the extraordinary becomes ordinary or the definition of values changes for a significant portion of the buying population, regardless of industry, that evolution can have its most sweeping impact on business. This type of value shift has happened three times over the past one hundred years. The first occurred at the turn of the century, the second around the sixties, and the third is happening right now.[26] With each successive evolutionary cycle, business models, the role of the customer, the point of value creation, and the drivers of profitability all changed quite dramatically (see table 1-2). In fact, the changes have been so significant that we tend to dub them "business revolutions." The fact is, however, there are no revolutions in business, only an unrecognized consumer evolution that changes the status quo. When you think about it this way, you can see that what customers value today has been building, or more accurately, evolving, for more than a hundred years.

The evolution of today's consumer values began with the Industrial Revolution, which made products available to the masses. In fact, the entire first half of the twentieth century could best be described as the

TABLE 1 - 2

Impact of the Evolution of Value on Business

	Early Consumerism (Early to Mid-1900s)	Transition Years (1960s–1990s)	New Millennium (2000 and Beyond)
Business focus	Company	Competition	Customer
Business model	Productivity	Market share or differentiation	Experiential value
Marketplace	Mass	Group	Individual
Customer role	Consumer	Customer	Participant
Point of value creation	Engineering and manufacturing	Engineering, manufacturing, and service	Entire company with customer as cocreator of value
Drivers of profitability	Cost and function	Volume, features, service, and quality	Experiences involving and surrounding product and company
Success metrics	Quantity of customers	Quantity of customers and customer satisfaction	Customer loyalty

"build it and they will come" era. Products were designed for and marketed to the masses with great success because almost every product offered was new, if not extraordinary. During this time, cost and function drove profitability, and value was created through the engineering and manufacturing of products that made life more convenient, comfortable, and exciting. Standout giants of this time were big companies such as Ford, General Motors, General Electric, Coca-Cola, and the Campbell Soup Company.

Eventually, though, the market became saturated with products and the consumer became more sophisticated and demanding. This heralded the second shift in value, which began in the early 1960s. Most economists refer to this as the service era, because consumers were beginning to look for value beyond the basic product. The name is somewhat misleading, however, because while service was certainly an important focus, quality and feature richness were also hallmarks of the time.

During this era consumers wanted more of a relationship with the companies they did business with as well. This was made possible by the advent of computers, which allowed businesses to keep more extensive records and manipulate data to create profiles and track patterns. The service era generated profits through volume sales and attracted customers with new features, service offerings, and claims of quality. Federal Express, IBM, and a redirected General Electric made their fortunes during this era.

As the evolutionary cycle continues, businesses find themselves once again dealing with consumers who want and expect something more than what they had in the past.[27] Consumption for the sake of consumption is no longer enough. Service that ignores the needs of the individual is no longer acceptable. Settling for the company's definition of value is a thing of the past. Customers no longer want to be treated like an audience watching a play, every line and movement controlled by the playwright. They want to be participants and cocreators of value, and they're getting their way.

Trying to satisfy this more sophisticated and complex consumer may seem an impossible task. Making a profit by delivering an individual consumer experience on a mass scale may seem equally impossible. But these goals are not out of reach. Any company that focuses on value can deliver the experiences customers seek, and they can do it today—just as soon as we answer this one simple question—what *is* experience?

PRICELESS ROADMAP—CHAPTER 1

- ➤ Identify the values your product or service currently offers by using a technique such as laddering.
- ➤ Identify which level each value impacts on the Value Model.
- ➤ Identify the unique Value Groups for your product or service.
- ➤ Evaluate your current marketing approach and identify whether you are clearly communicating your unique value.

CHAPTER two

When Is a Banana
Not a Banana?

THE VALUE EXPERIENCE

I N THE HEART OF THE FRENCH QUARTER IN New Orleans, a few friends and loyal patrons gathered in Owen Brennan's famous dining room. The year was 1951 and the occasion was the unveiling of a new recipe, an event the group had anticipated for weeks. Little did they know, however, it wasn't just a debut they were attending—it was the birth of a legend.

Warmed by candlelight, tantalized by the aroma of caramelized sugar mingling with cinnamon, the diners waited. When just the right mix of excitement and expectation was reached, Chef Paul Blange appeared. With a flourish he uncovered an arrangement of golden bananas nestled in an amber sauce. Placing the dish on a tableside burner, he bathed the fruit in rum, tipped the pan slightly forward, and in less time than it takes to blink, the creation burst into flames. Amid sounds of delight, the chef spooned the sizzling concoction over vanilla ice cream and watched as guests savored the first taste. The dessert was an immediate hit. People talked about it, critics wrote about it, and before long it became the signature dish at Brennan's. The name of this legendary dessert is Bananas

Foster, and as you might suspect, there's more to this story than meets the eye.

In 1950s New Orleans, bananas were cheap. As a primary port for importation from Central and South America, the supply far outweighed the local demand. In fact, the fruit was so plentiful people were actually bored with it. Owen Brennan, in addition to being an astute restaurateur, was also very involved in the economic growth of the city. At the moment, that meant pushing bananas. So when a local magazine asked Brennan to create a new recipe to premier in an article about his establishment, he saw a way to kill two birds with one stone. His instructions to Chef Blange were simple and straightforward—create anything you want as long as it's wonderful and made with bananas.

As we know, the chef came up with a way to do both, and in the end it served Brennan and New Orleans well. Even after fifty years, Bananas Foster is the most requested item on the restaurant's menu, using an astounding 35,000 pounds of flaming bananas a year.[1] Clearly, it's not just what you serve, but how you dish it up that matters. If Chef Blange had assembled Bananas Foster in the kitchen and served it like any other dessert, it might have been a success, but it's doubtful it would have been a legend. What makes the dish the classic it is today is the experience he created by combining the common elements of a recipe and presenting them in an uncommon way to tantalize and delight his customers.

This is what experience is all about—creating *reactions* in customers through their *interactions* with a product, a company, or its representatives. And because the very nature of commerce is to interact with customers, any company that offers goods or services to the marketplace creates hundreds of experiences every day. People shop for products, buy products, and use products. They clean and dispose of products. They arrange for service and talk to company representatives. Each of these is an experience that contributes to the value of an offering. Bananas Foster was a success because the dessert combined a tasty product with a flaming presentation that was not only satisfying but made diners feel special. This is the power of experience. It gives us the ability to delight our customers and add new dimensions to our offerings, transforming them from simply ordinary into extraordinary and even priceless.

In this chapter we'll probe the concept of experience—what it is and how it can be used to deliver value. We'll also discuss "experience events," those instances when customer interactions take place. You might be surprised how much even one unsatisfactory event can affect the value of an otherwise great product. Finally, we'll introduce you to the Value Experience. This is the ultimate prize, the priceless pinnacle that every company should strive for. To reach it, however, you have to expand your horizons beyond your company walls and your thinking beyond your product.

Experience 101

E XPERIENCE is a word we've heard many times during the past few years.[2] Commercials are rampant with it. Books and articles are being written about it. It's on the minds of sales and marketing people everywhere. But even though intuitively we know the consumer experience is important in today's world, how to create it remains elusive. The reason for this is not because it's so difficult to do, but because we don't clearly understand what we're trying to create.

So, in business terms, what *is* an experience?

First and foremost, an experience begins with an *interaction* between a customer and a product, a company, or its representative. So, by definition, *an experience cannot happen without the customer's involvement.* This is a critical point, because it requires a shift in thinking from consumers as customers to consumers as participants. You can't do it alone.

Once interaction takes place, a reaction occurs. In the case of Bananas Foster, the reaction was positive—one of delight. If the bananas had exploded at the table the reaction would have been negative, perhaps one of fear or shock. In either case, the result of the interaction was the formation of a feeling, an emotion.

Experiences can also result in thoughts. No one gets very emotional about interacting with laundry detergent, but if our clothes are clean, the experience registers as a favorable one in our minds. Therefore, interactions cause reactions, which manifest themselves as thoughts or feelings—both positive and negative. If a reaction is negative it detracts from the experience, but if it's positive, the experience registers value on one or more levels.

For example, the reaction to Bananas Foster was recognized on the physical level as pleasure. This is a predictable reaction. As long as a customer likes bananas or the spectacle of bananas on fire the dessert is bound to please. There is also the potential for other values to surface, however, depending on the person or the situation. In fact, what the customer brings to the table is as important as what the company is serving up. This is where experience gets interesting, but before we move on to the nuances of the subject, let's sum up the definition of experience we've been building to: *A consumer experience is an interaction or series of interactions between a customer and a product, a company, or its representative that lead to a reaction. When the reaction is positive, it results in the recognition of value.* This at least is the simple version. To really get to the heart of experience, however, you have to go deeper.

The Personal Touch

A N OIL PAINTING begins in the artist's imagination and using the tools at his disposal, it takes form on the canvas in a way no other human being on earth can duplicate. Each original is influenced by the history, emotions, preferences, and skill of the painter at the moment the painting is created. Experiences happen much the same way. Each individual brings his own values, beliefs, preferences, and history to an experience, making it unique.

Imagine two couples at Brennan's restaurant: One is an older couple, married many years and accustomed to dining at fine restaurants; the other is a young couple who indulge in an elegant dinner once or twice a year at great expense to their small budget. Both order Bananas Foster and both value the pleasure the dessert offers. The older couple, however, might also find intellectual value in the dessert. Since they dine in fine restaurants often, they have experienced many premium delicacies. This history gives them a basis for comparison. If Bananas Foster compares favorably, they will certainly register satisfaction and maybe even excellence.

The younger couple, on the other hand, will probably have a more emotional reaction. Sitting in an elegant dining room and receiving personal attention makes them feel special. Also, since this is an extraordinary evening in their eyes, the dessert experience will become part of their relationship history. We have two different couples who bring two different sets of personal dynamics to the experience; therefore they each receive different value. The older couple may register satisfaction, quality, excellence, and appreciation. The younger couple may experience satisfaction and appreciation, too, but they also receive value through a feeling of increased status, self-esteem, and a nurturing of their relationship.

Businesses often face the challenge of dealing with the individual tastes, preferences, and values a customer brings to an experience. You can honor these personal nuances, however, if you understand your customers. When you do, it's possible to anticipate their reactions and provide for their needs. One company that built a name on considering individuality and then delivering a very personal experience is Amazon.com.

Success, One Customer at a Time

Jeff Bezos, founder and CEO of Amazon.com, had a vision—to transport online bookselling back to the days of the small bookseller.[3] He knew this would be a challenge, because the virtual experience could never duplicate many of the experiences of the real world. "You'll never be able to hear the bindings creak and smell the books . . . and [sit in] soft sofas at Amazon.com," he admitted.[4] But even though he couldn't duplicate the atmosphere, he believed it was possible to replicate or even exceed the personal attention of the neighborhood store. Most agree that despite the fact that no one ever sees the face of a single Amazon.com employee, he did.

The secret to his success lies in the innovative use of technology and a singular focus to understand and serve each customer as an individual.

Let's say, for instance, you are a Stephen King fan. Once Amazon.com knows this, the company can not only notify you when a new title is coming out, but its editors can also suggest reading Peter Straub or Dean Koontz. If gardening or antique automobiles are more to your taste, the online experience allows you to see what other aficionados are reading and review their comments about books you're considering. Customers are also invited to participate in refining recommendations by rating purchases (just because you bought something doesn't mean you like it) and telling Amazon.com what other books, movies, or music you own and how you like them. These opportunities allow customers to better control their own experience, but even without these refinements the relational software Amazon.com employs is amazingly accurate at predicting what an individual will enjoy.

The company makes it easy for customers to tailor their experiences in other ways as well. For instance, readers can subscribe to newsletters on a variety of topics and genres from independent editors and independent presses. Amazon.com Delivers is another way customers can access recommendations, articles, and interviews on specific subjects. If a customer prefers a more passive approach, editors will e-mail recommendations directly to her and include a built-in link to her personalized Amazon.com home page in the message.

For buying customization, the online bookseller offers two choices. After building a profile, a customer can use one-click shopping to instantly process an order, bill it to a specified credit card, and have it shipped to a designated address. For multiple purchases, the shopping cart displays the customer's profile for easy order completion. At the bottom of the page, recent purchases are listed to help prevent duplicating an order by mistake. When the occasion calls for it, a customer can also choose gift-wrapping, send a personal note, or e-mail a gift certificate. No matter how diverse a customer's tastes might be or how he wants to make a purchase, ship, or communicate with Amazon.com, options are available to honor his individuality.

Serving people this way, on a customer-by-customer basis, has set the company apart from other merchants, both virtual and brick-and-mortar. This focus has also kept it alive despite a rocky road to profitability.

Many pundits and critics predicted the demise of Amazon.com for a variety of reasons, including what some consider a basically flawed business model. But the company is still around and finally profitable, because customers keep coming back—by the millions—each with her own quirks and preferences and each feeling as though her voice is heard. This enduring kind of success is what can happen when you find out what customers want, use this knowledge to anticipate their needs, take good care of them, and treat them as individuals. In the end they often stay with you—even when other circumstances change.

If the Circumstance Fits

IN ADDITION to the personal influences a customer brings to an experience, the context or the circumstances surrounding an experience can also be important. For example, a person wanting to grab a quick lunch before a one o'clock meeting will have a much different reaction to relaxed, leisurely service than someone using the lunch hour to take a break from the office. In the latter case, relaxed and leisurely is preferred, while our first person is probably tearing his hair out. Context, like the personal influences a customer brings to an experience, can be very individual.

Imagine you are a real estate agent and two different couples walk into your office. From all outward appearances they are identical, but their situations couldn't be more different. The first couple wants to build a new house sometime next year. Right now they're scouting out a location and house plans to fit their lifestyle requirements. Your second couple was just transferred to your area and needs to find a home right away. In each case the couple's situation influences their buying experience.

Because they are just beginning to evaluate their options for building a new home, the first couple needs information. So if the real estate agent, after assessing the situation and listening to their vision of a new home, tells the pair about developments in the area that fit their needs, that would be good. If he then offers brochures and house plans to take home for review, they will have an even better experience.

On the other hand, the second buyers need action. They want to make a quick purchase, desire a short closing period, and want everything processed quickly so they can settle in as soon as possible. They would place high value on an agent who could set up appointments right away and begin the prequalification process to expedite a loan. Two different customers, two different situations; how the agent deals with each will greatly affect the quality of their experience and the value they receive. Thus, in order to create the best possible experience, you not only have to understand the personal dynamics a customer brings to the table, but that person's situation as well. Armed with this information—the who and the why—your business can refine its Value Groups, anticipate the reactions of the customer, and even look for new ways to add value to an experience. But to do this, you first need to identify where value-enhancing opportunities exist.

Experience Events

A NY TIME a customer interacts with you, your product, or your representatives, that person is engaging in an experience. When you sell a product, you facilitate a buying experience. When you fix a copying machine, you deliver a repair experience. When someone at your company answers a phone, she begins a communication experience. Each of these experiences involves an interaction that has an opportunity to enhance value. The depth of that value depends largely on the success or failure of each event to produce the desired reaction. For instance, if a product works well, it will produce a favorable user experience, but if it were then difficult to dispose of, that would decrease the value of the offering. You need to identify the experience events surrounding your company's product and understand the impact each one has on the customer. When you do, the results can be surprising.

United States Surgical Corporation (U.S. Surgical) is a manufacturer and distributor of surgical supplies. After expanding globally, U.S. Surgical found its sales faltering. When it investigated the problem, it found the work force had become so disconnected and the sales process so slow and complex that it was negatively impacting business. The main reason for this disconnect was size: With more than three thousand products in inventory, it was difficult for the sales force to understand product specifications and determine pricing. As a result, 5.3 percent of orders were incorrectly priced, new contract setup time was three weeks, and it took more than two days to confirm an order.[5] This was not producing a good buying experience, to say the least.

In order to improve this glitch in the consumption process, U.S. Surgical implemented a sales force automation package and an intranet with marketing and product information. These tools allowed sales representatives to have ready access to the knowledge they needed to better serve the customer. Within a few months, incorrect orders were reduced to less than 1 percent, contract setup time to less than an hour, and order confirmation to about sixty minutes.[6] According to Jeffrey Sciallo, the company's vice president of information systems, customers were much happier because U.S. Surgical was more efficient and could respond to their needs more quickly. This initiative led to greater customer loyalty as well as reduced costs and higher productivity.[7] The enviable outcome was achieved not by focusing on the product, but on the buying experience.

Every manufactured good or service involves a myriad of events such as the buying experience that can add to or detract from the value of a product. Some are common; for example, most offerings must be purchased. Others are unique to a specific product or situation. Only someone with a broken arm will experience the removal of a cast. Plant maintenance and repair are unique to manufacturing or production facilities. Also, events can happen intermittently over a long period of time, or they may occur frequently and be over in a flash. For example, shopping for a car may take weeks and occur only every few years. Using a toothbrush takes only a few minutes but is repeated daily, offering endless opportunities to delight or annoy.

With all these variables it isn't the size, shape, number, duration, or repetition of an event that matters, but the impact it has on the consumer. Anyone who has ever purchased a personal computer can appreciate what we mean.

Out of the Blue

There's nothing quite like the experience of setting up a new PC. In fact, even though it might happen only once in a lifetime, it creates a lasting impression. What kind of impression is something IBM is trying to control.

Within the scope of high-pressure situations, installing a new computer has to rate near the top. The kids are waiting to surf the Net. The significant other wants to check e-mail, and about ninety minutes into the project you are reminded that the neighbor installed *his* PC in less than an hour. This of course is the same neighbor the family keeps suggesting you call for help. Meanwhile you're still trying to decipher manuals that appear to be written in a foreign language. It's the stuff nightmares are made of, but there is a ray of hope.

Over the past several years, a handful of PC manufacturers have finally acknowledged that setting up a computer, especially for their novice Value Group, is not a fun event. Working together under the direction of IBM's Ease of Use organization, the manufacturers took steps to improve what they called the out-of-box experience (OOBE). The group's first task was to identify the eight elements of the initial "hands-on" experience. These ranged from taking the computer out of the box to setup, configuration, and use: packaging, unpacking, setup, power on, configuration, initial use, doing work, and assistance. Next they identified key aspects of each element and developed guidelines or "best design practices" for each step to help improve the experience event.

For example, during setup, the computer invariably asks you a question well beyond your scope of understanding. Unsure of the correct answer, you—like most people—grab the manual and search for further explanation. While you are scanning the book for a possible answer, the system decides it has waited long enough, selects a default value, and continues through the installation process. At this point you don't know whether to turn the machine off and start again or if that will just make matters worse. This is a typical novice event—one that computer companies have always contended was impossible to predict.

Much to IBM's credit, however, it tackled many such issues and found solutions that could be addressed through product and procedure design. The result of its efforts was a set of guidelines and a point-weighted checklist that PC manufacturers could use to predict the outcome of a customer's initial experience with the product. Computers with high scores had fewer errors, faster setup times, and higher satisfaction ratings as validated by end-user performance testing.[8]

One of the first products developed using the OOBE design guidelines was the IBM NetVista X40, a distinctive computer whose difference is apparent as soon as you open the box.[9] The first item you encounter is a graphical setup poster detailing the installation process. This poster replaces the thick booklet most people found difficult or intimidating to use. Other innovations include simplified desktop organization and a one-click Update Connector that links users to a Web site with a list of updates available for download. The NetVista has won several awards, including *NetWork & Telecom*'s Reader's Choice Award.[10] But in our minds, its success is best described by the following proclamation in a *Miami Herald* article, "Oh what fun it is to own a computer."[11]

From nightmare to fun, not a bad return for focusing on one experience event and then making sure that every element contributes to making it a good one. What would happen if you did the same with all the experience events surrounding a product? You would have something very special indeed.

The Value Experience

IMAGINE THIS SCENARIO: You check into a hotel and your favorite beverage is chilling in your room, dinner reservations have been confirmed, and a robe in exactly your size is laid out on the bed. During your stay, your phone messages are hand delivered and your favorite morning drink and a newspaper are waiting outside your door when you wake up. At checkout, your flight has been confirmed, your ride to the airport is waiting, and along with your bill you receive a small gift in appreciation for your business. You gladly sign the bill; in fact, you look forward to your next visit. Seem like a dream? It isn't; it's a Value

Experience—a product or service that when combined with its surrounding experience events goes beyond itself to enhance or bring value to a customer's life.

This is the ideal that *Priceless* embodies—to deliver such overall value that a product transcends the ordinary to become extraordinary or even priceless. It is what customers are looking for and what every business should strive to deliver, regardless of what it sells. In previous pages we've already uncovered some of the knowledge you'll need to deliver this prize. For instance, in chapter 1, we learned about the nature of value and its impact on the whole being—physical, emotional, intellectual, and spiritual. The Value Model was also introduced to help identify individual and group values as well as evaluate products and services to determine the value they offer. We also explored the evolution of value to uncover what consumers are seeking today—rich experiences that touch every level of their being. Another piece of the puzzle fell into place with the examination of experience, when we learned that interactions during experience events cause customer reactions, which lead to a judgment of value. Our final task is to understand how these judgments stack up in terms of value. With this insight we can determine if a customer is on her way to a Value Experience or in for another dose of the ordinary. The key to this insight is understanding rewards and sacrifices.

Give and Take

E ARLIER IN THE CHAPTER we made the point that experience is interactive and the customer is obviously a participant in each experience. This view of consumption recognizes the fact that the customer, not just the company, brings something to the experience table. We already know that part of what customers contribute stems from their personal dynamics and their unique situations. But we must also recognize that customers make other contributions as well. When customers make a purchase, they expend time, effort, money, thought, emotion, and so forth. In exchange for these contributions, people expect value. Or, we might say that in exchange for their *sacrifices*, they expect *rewards*. In order to create the best Value Experience, you need to limit the sacrifices and increase the rewards. Let's see how this works.

A salesman named Tony just landed an appointment with the CEO he's been courting for the past three months. Wanting to look his best, he decides it's time for a haircut but he hasn't been happy with the salon he's used in the past. Based on the strong recommendation of a friend, Tony decides to try Vaughn's. On his first attempt to make an appointment, the line is busy. Tony tries again later and then later again. On the fourth try he finally connects, but his annoyance over the appointment-making experience is only slightly lessened when the receptionist tells him she can squeeze him in on Monday with Samantha.

When Monday arrives, Tony shows up ten minutes early—good thing, because the line is so long that it takes several minutes to check in. He finds this surprising as his friend had specifically mentioned the salon's great service. When he's finally seated in the shampoo chair, he really needs the scalp massage included with the service. The experience is relaxing, so when he reaches Samantha, he's happy to chat with her while she cuts his hair. The conversation is pleasant and she's efficient, so it doesn't take long to finish up, something Tony appreciates. Feeling content, he leaves her a nice tip and proceeds to check out. Then he sees another long line.

This roller coaster of feelings is not unusual in a series of experience events. So how do we know if the sum of events is enough to deliver a Value Experience? One way to determine the overall impact of individual events is to map them to an experience event matrix. On this matrix, events can score in one of three categories: rewards, sacrifices, or neutral. Rewards are based on value received. If a product offers convenience, that is a reward. *Rewards always add to the value of an experience.* You can refer to the Value Model to help identify possible values your company offers. Sacrifices, on the other hand, require effort or payout on the part of the customer. Driving to the store is a sacrifice. Having to take off work or reschedule the day's appointments around a repair call is a sacrifice. *Sacrifices always decrease the value of an experience.* A neutral event, however, is one that neither increases nor decreases value. An example of a neutral event might be putting the teakettle on to make tea. It really doesn't increase or decrease value; it is simply an event in the process of consuming tea. Now if the teakettle were hard to fill, that might be a sacrifice, but in general this event doesn't have much impact. First, then, you need to determine if an event is a reward, sacrifice, or neutral.

The next step is to identify the impact a reward or sacrifice has on the customer—low, medium, or high. Low impact occurs when something is expected by the customer and therefore either *ordinary* in the case of a reward, or *acceptable* in the case of a sacrifice. We expect to have to check in at a rental car counter to rent a car. This is an acceptable sacrifice. We expect fast service at McDonald's so when that's what we get, it's a reward, just not an extraordinary one. To move from ordinary to extraordinary, there has to be value beyond what is normally expected.

For example, there is no waiting in line when you sign up as a preferred customer at Hertz. When you arrive at the rental car lot, your name is listed on a board along with the space number for your car's location. When you arrive at the car, usually only steps away from the drop-off point, the trunk is open and the rental agreement is sitting on the front seat. When the weather is cold, the car is running with the heater on. With this level of service, the picking-up-the-rental-car experience delivers a greater reward than expected; therefore it registers as medium impact and an extraordinary experience. On the other hand, if you arrive at a rental car counter and the line is three blocks long and it takes an hour to complete the process, this would be a medium impact and an unacceptable sacrifice. Companies should constantly monitor their experience events to make sure they are offering as many significant rewards as possible while limiting sacrifices.

Let's return to Tony for a moment and see how his experience would fare on the experience event matrix. Rewards for Tony included the scalp massage, Samantha's personal attention, and a nice haircut. Two out of three of these rewards score above ordinary because they were unexpected. The cut was nice, but given the salon's reputation, he expected no less. So we would give that a low impact reward. The sacrifices he encountered were a busy phone line, waiting several minutes to check in, and a long checkout line. All of these sacrifices were unacceptable. Tony went in expecting excellent service and in fact got the opposite, so he wasn't at all happy about the final sacrifice he had to make—paying a premium price (see figure 2-1). So the matrix tells us Tony's experience had one ordinary and two extraordinary rewards, three unacceptable and one intolerable sacrifice. If you were to assign a number value to each of the categories ranging from one to three points (one being ordinary and acceptable), then sacrifice points outweighed reward points nine to five. Based on this outcome, Tony did not receive a Value Experience. In fact, the whole affair didn't even register as ordinary (when reward and sacrifice points are equal), so Vaughn's should not expect Tony to return.

This outcome is unfortunate, because the salon has a good product and it wouldn't take much more than better management of the appointment and front desk processes to alter the experience. If you recognize

FIGURE 2 - 1

Hair Salon Experience Event Matrix

	Low	Medium	High
Reward	Ordinary Haircut	Extraordinary Massage Personal attention	Priceless
Neutral	Has Little or No Impact		
Sacrifice	Acceptable	Unacceptable Busy phone Check-in Checkout	Intolerable

Source: Adapted from the ACE Matrix developed by Ian C. MacMillan and Rita Gunther McGrath. Reprinted by permission of Harvard Business Review. From "Discover Your Products' Hidden Potential" by Ian C. MacMillan and Rita Gunther McGrath, Harvard Business Review, May–June 1996, 5.

that your customers are being subjected to unacceptable or intolerable sacrifices, you may be able to transform them into rewards. Every company, no matter how large or small, has been guilty of delivering substandard value at one time or another. It happens. What's important is to recognize when customers have made an unacceptable sacrifice and then do something about it. In 1994 the Walt Disney Company found itself in just such a situation, and handled it in classic Disney style.[12]

If at First You Don't Succeed

With the Christmas season just ahead, Disney proudly introduced an interactive CD-ROM version of its popular movie *The Lion King*. On Christmas morning thousands of children delighted in the gift, but their excitement soon vanished when, later in the day, frustrated parents with little computer experience were unable to install the software. Not anticipating a serious problem with this particular product, the company was shocked when an understaffed hot line was flooded with angry calls from parents of disappointed children. This clearly was a case of an unacceptable sacrifice.

The following Christmas, Disney offered another interactive CD, this one based on the *Pocahontas* movie. Needless to say, the major technical difficulties that had caused problems the previous year were eliminated. But Disney wasn't taking any chances. This year the company designed the product with the context of Christmas morning in mind. Each *Pocahontas* CD-ROM arrived with instructions addressed to parents. These instructions advised moms and dads to open, install, and learn to use the software *before* Christmas morning. If parents encountered problems, they could solve them—calmly—before the big day arrived. Special wrapping was also included so the package could be rewrapped and the little ones would be none the wiser.

The lesson we can take from the entertainment giant is that it's never too late to turn a sacrifice into a reward or a series of events into a Value Experience. In fact, you might be able to take sacrifices people are accustomed to making and turn them into substantial rewards. Caltex

Petroleum, a Texaco subsidiary in Africa, had always taken pride in its clean restroom facilities, but this was not the industry norm. For the most part, gas station restrooms in the area were dirty and unsightly, so much so that vacationing families did what they could to avoid them. Realizing this, Caltex turned an industry-wide sacrifice into a company-specific reward by advertising the fact that its restrooms were always clean. This happy circumstance encouraged people to buy gasoline where they also felt comfortable taking a bathroom break. Turning this sacrifice into a reward not only served the customer well and increased business for Caltex, but also made the competition's standards go from accept-able—it's like that everywhere—to unacceptable.[13]

Every day businesses are faced with opportunities to deliver rewards and limit sacrifices in this and many other ways. In making decisions about design, production, service, distribution, marketing, and many other factors that affect the customer experience, it's critical that you're aware of what those decisions mean to the customer. Will interactions with your product, your company, and its representatives result in positive or negative reactions? Will the events you set in motion represent sacri-fices or rewards?

Is your company prepared to deliver a Value Experience?

If it isn't now, it needs to be soon. The Value Experience is to today's business world what quality was to our counterparts in the 1970s and 1980s. During that era companies that offered inferior quality suffered fi-nancially and watched as market share declined—sometimes to zero.[14] Companies today that don't offer value to their customers will suffer the same fate. It's not an option. Evolution shows us that now is the time. Customers tell us now is the time. And we are telling you, now is the time. If you don't deliver a Value Experience your competition will, at your expense. In the remainder of the book we'll show you how to make the transition from a company that merely sells goods or services to one that delivers a Value Experience. But first we'd like to leave you with a story about one small business that has already made the transition in an industry that few think of as value-oriented. We believe if it can make value an everyday part of its enterprise, anyone can.

A Healthy Experience

Health care is a tough field to be in these days. Insurance companies dictate fees and patients are shuffled from one plan to another, often losing trusted doctors along the way. If a patient belongs to an HMO, as many do today, he or she sometimes can't even see a specialist without a referral and a long wait to get an appointment. It is a frustrating experience often compounded by the fact that the patient is just plain sick. To help their customers navigate the system and in the process help themselves cope as well, a group of doctors in northeastern Illinois formed the Deerpath Medical Associates. With specialists ranging from allergists to ophthalmologists aligned with the group, there is very little a patient will find lacking. What really sets Deerpath apart, however, is its focus on making it easy to be cared for.

Every morning, Monday through Saturday, its offices open at 7:00 A.M. For the next forty-five minutes, any patient can walk in and sign up to see a doctor that morning. Earaches, sore throats, nasty coughs, and strained muscles from an overambitious workout are common complaints for these walk-in sessions. To handle the load, two or three doctors from the group are assigned each morning to see patients. They work efficiently, turning examination rooms over every fifteen minutes.

Imagine coming home from work with a scratchy throat or climbing into bed with a fever, knowing you can see a doctor the next morning without even having to make a phone call. It's comforting and it's good medicine. Because patients can easily access a physician six days a week, they are less likely to self-doctor or wait until a minor ailment becomes a serious illness. They are also less likely to jump ship for a group that doesn't offer such convenience.

Deerpath takes the hassle out of health care in other ways as well. During scheduled appointments, the wait to see the doctor is rarely more than ten minutes. Each patient chart has an updated summary page, so doctors know the pertinent history when they walk in the examining room. If a referral is necessary, the office sends it to the specialist or testing facility, often the same day, then puts a copy of it in the mail for your records. The patient doesn't have to handle the paperwork as they do with many other HMOs. The patient can access routine test results within three days via a password-protected messaging center. Doctors and nurses record the messages themselves, so they're personal and nonthreatening. If results need to be discussed, the doctor makes a personal call. It's very smooth and requires very little effort on the part of the patient.

This focus on making it easy to be cared for allows patients to concentrate on their health, not their health care provider. It's remarkable really, as though the doctors stepped into their customer's shoes and walked through each experience event to determine the best way to deliver value. What do you think would happen if you did the same with your own company? Would each interaction with your customer add up to a Value Experience? The only way to know for sure is to walk the path your customers take every day. That's where we're headed next.

PRICELESS ROADMAP—CHAPTER 2

> Identify common customer situations that might influence how customers interact with your product or service.

> Identify opportunities to increase value for each type of customer situation.

> Select a customer experience that currently registers as an ordinary reward and brainstorm ways to change its impact to extraordinary or priceless.

> Select an experience event that currently registers as a sacrifice and brainstorm ways to turn it into a neutral impact or a reward.

CHAPTER three

The Journey Begins

THE EXPERIENCE
ENGAGEMENT PROCESS

O N AUGUST 15, 1998, MILLIONS OF AMERICANS watched as a close-up of a wall outlet and phone jack filled their TV screens. This curious picture was followed by a disembodied hand plugging in first a power cord and then a phone line. "Presenting three easy steps to the Internet," a voice announced. "Step one, plug-in . . . step two, get connected." As the screen faded to a rotating view of Apple's new iMac computer, the voice continued, "Step three" (quiet laughter). "There's not a step three . . . there's no step three" (more quiet laughter).[1]

With that commercial, the iMac mantra—simple to set up and simple to use—was broadcast around the world. And the world, or at least a generation of young people and their technophobic parents, was listening. Built from the ground up with the masses in mind, this was a computer for the computer-illiterate. Anyone from a seventy-year-old grandmother to a six-year-old kindergartner could use it with minimal instruction. What's more, with its lollipop colors and strategically placed clear panels revealing its inner workings, the iMac wasn't the least bit scary. Finally, the Internet was accessible to anyone with $1,000 and a desire to surf. But the fact that the product did exactly what it professed to do was only part of its success. The real reason the iMac put Apple Computer back on the business map is that the company never lost sight of its true purpose—to help people get online quickly and easily.

From the start, Apple engineers made sure the iMac's Internet software and instructions for connection were as understandable as possible. Files weren't buried in an obscure electronic folder on something called a "C drive," and setup procedures didn't ask confusing questions like what kind of modem one was using. Instead, the engineers eliminated much of the guesswork and with it most of the fear, but they didn't stop there. Apple also developed a suite of multimedia tools to enrich the computing experience. Imagine being able to convert CDs to virtual jukeboxes or create and edit digital movies right in your home. Now people could do all of the cool things their geekier friends were talking about. They could even post their accomplishments on a community Web site. Apple saw their need and gave them exactly what they wanted, exactly how they wanted it, every step of the way.

Within three months of launch, the iMac accounted for 7.1 percent of PC unit sales, beating out the Compaq Presario 5150 as the top-selling PC. In the first six months, Apple shipped 278,000 units and doubled its market share among consumers to nearly 10 percent. More important, independent research showed that 40 percent of the buyers were first-time Apple customers and 29.4 percent first-time computer users. Apple reported its first full-year profit since 1995 because of the iMac. In a world where 70 percent of new products fail, Apple achieved the equivalent of putting a man on the moon. And it did so by creating a great product *and* a great experience from start to finish. It is this start-to-finish process that plays such an important role in creating a Value Experience.[2]

In chapter 2 we explored how a Value Experience occurs when a series of rewarding events combine to deliver overall value to the customer. We also discovered that events sometimes fall short of expectations, creating at best an ordinary experience. This being the case, it's crucial that we understand each event surrounding an offering and the impact it has on the customer. For this insight we turn to the Experience Engagement Process (EEP).

Adapted from a consumer decision-making model developed by Johan Arndt, the Experience Engagement Process consists of five stages —*discover, evaluate, acquire, integrate,* and *extend*—through which the customer moves during consumption.[3] By examining these stages, a business can see rewards and sacrifices through its customers' eyes, thus uncovering the real value of an offering. For most companies this exercise is a real eye-opener.

As we examine the different stages, keep in mind that not all consumers will go through every stage each time. For instance, the owner of a Hewlett-Packard printer who always buys HP replacement cartridges won't reevaluate the purchase each time, nor will buying manufactured goods involve the same events as services. Nonetheless, understanding what happens during each stage will help you chart the best possible course toward a Value Experience.

Stage One—Discover

E VERY PURCHASE must have a beginning, that first impulse to buy that sets the consumption experience in motion. This impulse may be company-induced—for instance, the iMac commercial inspires someone to join the Internet age. It can be self-induced—a woman decides she needs a new pair of shoes. Or it can be situation-induced—the copying machine breaks down. However it begins, the consumer uses the discover stage to *identify products and services to meet specific wants and needs and to uncover possible sources for them.* Businesses have traditionally viewed this stage primarily as a time to persuade, entice, and even seduce consumers into buying products and services through advertising and promotion. But as we'll see, providing a good discover experience takes more than snappy patter and slick images.

In the United States today, consumers are inundated with literally billions of "discover messages." In fact, some believe we're suffering from information overload.[4] The reason for this profusion of discovery opportunities stems from the fact that most marketing and advertising is geared toward the first type of discovery—company-induced discovery.[5] This method attempts to convince people they want something before they even know they want it. When this is done in a mass-market sort of way—casting the message out to anyone and everyone, hoping for a few nibbles—it just adds to the clutter. When marketing is done well and is targeted to the needs (whether actual or perceived) of a significant Value Group, it is effective and even appreciated by the consumer. Let's look at Apple and the iMac commercials again, this time in light of the discover process.

In 1998 there were hundreds of thousands of people who wanted to be online, but the technology was so intimidating they stayed away from it. The initial iMac commercials assured them they had nothing to fear. Apple clearly demonstrated how easy it was to use—1, 2, 3 easy—and what being online could bring to people's lives. Parents didn't have to be afraid to buy a computer for their teenagers, because they didn't have to endure a complicated installation process. Teens didn't have to be afraid to ask for a computer because they knew their parents could cope. In subsequent ads Apple featured other aspects of Internet use that iMac facilitated. Grandparents could see instant pictures of their grandkids and moms could communicate with their college kids. Apple appealed to the heart, the mind, and the child in everyone while killing the boogeyman at the same time. The approach was effective because it was personal and supportive of the kind of experience people were looking for.

To succeed in the discover stage, you have to be like Apple and make it easy for consumers to ascertain the value of your offering.[6] If you don't, you risk going *un*discovered. For instance, an ad for the RCA Scenium 65" Diagonal HDTV featured a graphic we think was meant to portray the coming together of a super-model and a rocket scientist. We're not sure why. As a discover experience, the ad was largely ineffective because the most visable aspects of the ad—the headline and the graphic—failed to communicate the value of the product. The ad's one saving grace was a lone sentence buried in the body copy; it said the television "takes your senses to the movie theatre and gives them front row seats."[7] This paints a great picture that could attract movie buffs and give them a reason to spend thousands of dollars, but they really had to dig for it. After spending so much effort and money on advertising, it's unfortunate when a company misses the chance to reach a buyer—especially if that buyer has already decided to make a purchase.

People in this group represent our second type of consumer—buyers with a self-induced impulse to acquire something new. When trying to reach this group, your goal isn't to create an impulse to buy but rather to help the consumer discover the value of your product. For example, Jenifer wakes up one morning and decides to redecorate her house. Spring is on the way, and after a long winter, she's ready for a change. There are several ways this customer can approach the discover stage. She can look in the phone book for a decorator who will coordinate everything for her, but using a professional will cut into her decorating budget. So that's out. She can go to stores she's shopped at before for furniture, paint, and home accessories and see what they have, although this will mean several stops. Or, she can try a new place she's driven by on her way to work called the Great Indoors. The big, impressive building looks as though it will have everything she needs. Just to make sure, though, she pops online to check it out.

From the very first look, Jenifer knows she's discovered a treasure. The Web site's tag line reads, "The place for people who love to decorate, redecorate and remodel." That's her. A clever little ad on the home page asks, "Do you stay in nice hotels to get away from it all or get ideas for your bathroom? There's a place for people like you."[8] This also sounds like Jenifer. The clincher, though, is an invitation to create great kitchens, great baths, great bedrooms, and great rooms with their help. Without looking further, Jenifer heads for the Great Indoors.

Sears, the power behind this innovative interior design store, did several things right in attracting this customer who was already in the mood to buy. First of all, the name is descriptive of the value people will gain by doing business with the store—creating a great living environment. Even from a busy highway, it is apparent what the Great Indoors is all about. Second, it has an easy-to-find Web site, and it advertises where people on an interior design quest are likely to look, such as decorating and home magazines. The final draw is the store concept itself. Decorating, redecorating, and remodeling are almost always a customer-induced impulse, but many components are involved. By assembling everything its Value Groups need to create personalized indoor spaces under one roof, the store makes discovery very easy.

To facilitate the discover process for consumers who have already decided to purchase, businesses should determine where consumers will look when the impulse to buy occurs. This might be the Internet, publications targeted to the specific context of the purchase (such as *Interior Design* in the case of the Great Indoors), a local phone book, or a retail center such as a mall. If you're a manufacturer, be sure your advertising tells people where they can buy your product. There's nothing more frustrating than learning about the perfect product only to be left on one's own to locate it. Remember, this consumer has already decided to buy, so your job is to make it possible to act on that impulse.

Sometimes it's not the buyer but the situation that creates a need to buy and sets the discover process in motion. When you know your customers well and understand the value your product brings to them, you can anticipate events that might occur in their lives and target your marketing accordingly. As a health care product manufacturer, Johnson & Johnson wants consumers to think of their product, rather than a competitor's when they have a headache. So, the company has found creative ways of placing itself at the right place and the right time. For instance, when the stock market falls by more than one hundred points, banner ads for Tylenol unfurl on e-broker sites across the World Wide Web—a subtle reminder that in stressful times a Tylenol can help ease a nervous broker's situation. This is not only an efficient use of J&J's advertising dollars, but a great example of putting a product in front of a customer when it's needed the most.[9]

Knowing when, where, and how to put your offerings in front of the customer is key to creating an effective discovery experience. Consumers today are so inundated with advertising and promotion that they've become blind to much of it and are often unimpressed by what they do notice. In *Soul of the New Consumer*, Lewis and Bridger tell us that people are increasingly "able to spot the strategies behind advertisement, with the result that conventional methods of persuasion often fail to move them."[10] To attract today's consumer, the discover phase must be less about the offerings themselves and more about the Value Experiences those goods and services can provide. This is true in any market and with any type of customer, no matter where the impulse to buy begins. Your job will always be to facilitate discovery by speaking directly to the fit between your product or service and the value your customers are seeking. Once you have their attention, you can move them to the next phase of the Experience Engagement Process.

Stage Two—Evaluate

MANY have called the last decade the Information Age, and to some extent, that's true. So much information is produced today that as a society we are literally overwhelmed by it.[11] However, it isn't the availability of information itself that has changed the business world, but what that information enables, especially in terms of consumption. Consumers today are able to gather volumes of information on almost any company, product, or service they want. Using sources like the Internet, labels, consumer reports, articles, and even advertising, they scrutinize, compare, study, and weigh the options before making a decision.[12] This is the purpose of the evaluate stage—to examine the possible choices discovered in stage one and narrow them down to a single winner. Whether or not that winner is your company depends a great deal on how well you communicate the Value Experience you offer versus that of a competitor. If what you promise is right for the customer, she may well choose to buy from you. And it can help clinch the deal if you are the one who makes the evaluation stage a rewarding experience.

Subtle Persuasion

Pharmacia, developers of the hair-loss treatment Rogaine, was facing the expiration of its exclusive patent on its first-to-market formula. Competitors were already waiting in the wings and alternative treatments were cropping up everywhere. At the same time, the once prescription-only treatment was now available over the counter. Although this resulted in easier access to a larger number of people, it also meant the company lost an entire fleet of knowledgeable salespeople when doctors were no longer in the picture. In order to shore up its position as the market leader and exert as much control as possible over the evaluation process, Pharmacia turned to the Internet. Using technology, it hoped to make it easier for people to evaluate the benefits of its product and at the same time either close the sale online or drive customers to the store convinced Rogaine was the best choice.[13]

Recognizing that hair loss is a very personal issue and therefore comes with intimate concerns and questions, the company's first order of business was to make it comfortable for visitors to learn more about this painful subject. On entering the site, visitors are invited to click into either the men's or women's center, where each will find information geared specifically for his or her needs and interests. To offer even more specialized value, educational material is grouped not only by gender, but also by the type and level of information. For instance, in the men's section, one information path is geared for those just beginning their search for a hair-loss treatment; another leads directly to an area for longtime Rogaine users. Our examination focused on the prospective buyer.

In dealing with prospects, Pharmacia understands that a man exploring treatment options for hair loss needs more than product details. Often this consumer wants to know about the cause of his condition. The Rogaine site offers expertly prepared information about the various causes of baldness and statistics that assure visitors they are among a growing segment of the population. A section called "Men and Their Hair" discusses the psychological effects of balding as well as styling tips for thinning hair. Different treatment options such as hair transplants and wigs are also presented. Obviously, since it is Pharmacia's site, Rogaine has the most visibility, but the fact that the company is genuinely trying to educate, not just sell, gives Pharmacia added credibility as an objective expert in the field. The visitor now associates Pharmacia with authoritative, well-rounded information, even if he doesn't buy immediately.

The women's section also offers a wealth of information, but because the product's availability to women is fairly recent, it is geared primarily toward those just beginning their treatment search. Much of the information is the same as that presented in the men's section, but from a female viewpoint. When addressing men, the issue of hair loss is approached from a clinical standpoint. The women's content, however, is presented as part of the beauty regime, placing it in a familiar context to which women can easily relate. A community aspect to the site is particularly well developed in the women's section: Through forums, e-mail, and message boards, women can seek expert advice from stylists, dermatologists, psychologists, and product specialists on various treatment options. There are also community forums where customers can talk to each other about alternatives. The sheer volume of information and assistance available throughout the site is impressive and productive—something that would not have been possible ten years ago. The Internet has made it feasible for almost any company to increase the value of its offering during the evaluation stage. In fact, we believe providing the means to evaluate buying choices is one of the best ways a company can use the Internet.

Of course, technology isn't the only way people evaluate a product or service. They still pick up brochures; call or write for information; ask families, friends, and colleagues for advice; or just head to a store for a hands-on comparison. What is different today from a decade ago, however, is the fact that people often ask more questions and expect more in-depth answers.[14] This is even true when, as is often the case in a business environment, the evaluation stage involves a dealer channel.

Try Before You Buy

The meteoric rise in the use of technology in business has brought incredible opportunities as well as challenges to component manufacturers—especially those who produce parts for complex systems. Cisco Systems, the worldwide leader in networking for the Internet, is one of these. Its products help transport data, voice, and video within buildings, across town, and around the world. However, Cisco products are only one component of a complex and highly individual computing architecture. The challenge, therefore, is how to enable a potential customer to evaluate the merit of Cisco products when they can be truly tested only as part of a complete environment. The answer was found in Cisco's own labs.

So many components comprise today's complex computer systems, it's impossible to predict exactly what type of architecture an environment will have in any given company. Thus, in order to make sure its products work in any situation, Cisco labs can replicate different configurations and scenarios. Recognizing the benefit of such customization in the evaluation stage, Cisco created demonstration labs that resellers and their customers can use to see how Cisco products will function in their particular environment. Working with Cisco experts, the customer can set up a network exactly as wanted and see it at work before making a costly investment.[15] The lab is much more impressive and effective in demonstrating value than handing a customer a folder full of technical data that may or may not pertain to an individual situation.

The Great Indoors has also taken advantage of technology inside its stores to make selecting furniture easier. Using computer terminals, customers can "build" a room with the same dimensions as their own and "place" furniture in it to see how it will work in their space. This helps people avoid mistakes, at least in size, and allows them to visualize the furnishings in a room before they buy. To make the evaluate stage a rewarding part of the Experience Engagement Process, you have to provide the right information in the right format for your Value Groups and be there when questions arise. If the value you offer is the value they seek and you help them recognize it, you have a good chance to make a sale.

Stage Three—Acquire

E VERY CUSTOMER, no matter who he is or where he shops, eventually comes to the acquire stage. This is the point at which goods and services are actually purchased. On the surface, this seems simple, but in real life it often isn't. In fact, the sheer number of events involved in making a purchase (such as locating vendors, parking, ordering, and paying), can make acquisition one of the most complex and sacrifice-laden legs of the consumption journey. A case in point: A year or so ago a friend told Diana about a line of kitchen utensils by OXO called Good Grips. She raved about how comfortable the products were, so when Diana's old metal can opener bit the dust, it gave her an excuse to give the brand a try. On her next visit to Bed, Bath & Beyond, she sought out her target and found not only a Good Grips can opener, but an entire wall of the company's stylish utensils. At first she was excited, but she soon realized the wall was easily twelve feet high and the can opener was hanging at least two-thirds of the way up. At last check she was not seven feet tall.

Now she had a choice to make. Spend time tracking down an associate, scale a wall of kitchen utensils with her bare hands, or buy some other, less heavenly brand located closer to earth. Since time was running short and it was really just a can opener, she decided to pass and bought a competitor's product. Here was a case where a company had a customer ready to buy but its retailer threw a roadblock in the acquire stage. It's safe to say this is not what OXO wanted, but if the company had focused on the acquisition event from the customer's perspective, it would have spotted this problem before a sale was needlessly lost. Unfortunately, many producers of goods and services fail to recognize that retailer shortcomings such as inaccessible products, poor parking, and long checkout lines are problems related to *their* customer's experience.

In the movie *You've Got Mail,* the Tom Hanks character tells a small shop owner (Meg Ryan) who is forced to close her business because of his big superstore, "It's not personal, it's business." She replies, "Well it sure is personal to me." If you get nothing else from this book, please remember that everything you or anyone related to your product does to the customer is very personal. Whatever you can do to eliminate sacrifices will have a great impact. The process of acquiring a product or service yields almost limitless opportunities to create rewards or sacrifices. In fact, if your company focused on this stage alone and left the others until later, you would probably see your business increase. After all, if the customer has trouble buying your offering, any other work you do is wasted. Therefore, it's imperative that you know exactly what is involved in the acquisition stage and how each event impacts the Value Experience.

In order to acquire a product, consumers need to exert some effort. They have to make an appointment, locate a store, or place an order. Next they may need to drive to the location and find a parking space, log on to a Web site, or track down a salesperson. Once the desired product is located—sometimes an adventure in itself—a person has to wait in line to check out, pay for it, and take the purchase home. Services are slightly different, but consumers still have to make appointments, check in, wait, pay, and so on. Anywhere along the way you, your representatives, or distribution chain can add to or detract from value.

Speedy Rewards

Let's imagine it's Thursday afternoon and your spouse calls to ask you to pick up a carton of milk, a rotisserie chicken, and a bottle of Tylenol at the grocery store on your way home. When six o'clock rolls around you take two side roads hoping to avoid some traffic, but it still takes almost ten minutes to get through a single stoplight. When the grocery store finally comes into view, you see the parking lot is nearly full, so you take the first space you find, telling yourself it's a nice day for a walk.

Inside, the store is bustling with shoppers, some on small errands and others maneuvering overloaded carts through the aisles. Working your way through the crowds, you retrieve the requested items and join a long line of fellow express-lane buyers. While shifting from side to side, you see a store employee waving you toward four wonderfully empty checkout lanes partially hidden by a tall stack of diet soda. Taking the basket from you, the pleasant employee explains that you are her first customer for the store's new U-Scan express lanes. She describes the process for scanning your own groceries and then waves your chicken over the scanner. The purchase registers on a screen with a description and price. As you try it yourself, a pleasant computer voice guides you through the touch-screen prompts. You then bag your items and pay by cash, credit, or debit card. The payment process is really nothing new: U-Scan accepts bills and coins like soft-drink vending machines do, and the card swipes are the same as those at the end of most regular checkout lanes. The whole process has taken maybe three minutes and you're ready to go. Now if someone could just bring you your car.

This story is not a fantasy. Kroger, the nation's largest grocery chain with more than 2,300 supermarkets in thirty-one states, has been rolling out the self-serve lanes over the past three years. With express lanes now in more than two hundred locations, the company says customers love the convenience and grocers love the labor-saving efficiency. Four U-Scan lanes require only one attending employee versus the one or two required for traditional lanes. The point, however, says Kroger's, is not to replace people, but simply to supplement express-lane service and ease one step in the acquisition process.[16] Our short grocery store excursion took us through four different acquisition events—driving, parking, shopping, and paying—three of which the company can control, so it has the opportunity to minimize sacrifices and enhance rewards within its own system. The next story has fewer events, but the overall acquisition stage still had tremendous impact on the customer's perception of value.

Choices

Companies often buy service contracts on expensive or critical equipment to protect their business in case of a failure. Most agree this protection is necessary, but sometimes keeping up with renewals and new equipment can be a nightmare. When dcVAST, an IT services and consulting company, found that many of its customers were having difficulties managing the purchase of their contract coverage from multiple vendors, it offered a service to help companies buy the right service at the right time.

The program works by first analyzing all of the customer's technology contracts. Eligible hardware and software, service levels, length of coverage, and expiration dates are all inventoried. A team of service specialists then matches each piece of equipment with the level of service needed for its use, age, and so forth and recommends the proper coverage. "Often without even thinking, a company buys the highest level of service available, even though that level of coverage is only needed on 60 percent of the equipment," says Don Swanson, dcVAST CEO. "The programs are just too complex and take too much time to understand, so people err on the high side."[17]

Another problem is keeping track of equipment use and expiration dates. "We've found retired equipment sitting in a storeroom with expensive levels of service. Once we even discovered a computer with two separate contracts for the same coverage," said Swanson. "It's not really surprising given the way manufacturers structure their agreements. In many cases, contracts can only be sold for twelve months or longer. This means that if a company is actively buying all year, each procurement becomes another service contract. With one customer, we determined they had a service contract expiring every two days."[18]

Since dcVAST can sell manufacturer-delivered service as well as its own, it is able to help the customer set the proper service levels for each asset, then work with the manufacturer to bring all of the contracts under one umbrella with a common expiration date. This consolidation usually takes place over a year's time, because as each contract expires, it has to be brought under the umbrella. As new equipment is purchased it can also be added to the contract. "Customers usually save 10 to 30 percent depending on how diligent their people have been with buying the right service levels," says Swanson. "But for most of them it's not even the money savings they're the most excited about. It's the feeling of having regained control—or as one customer said, it feels good to be managing my contract purchases instead of them managing me."[19]

This issue of control is an important part of the acquisition experience, especially today. Since the Internet has shown consumers how rewarding it can be to shop where and when they want, they have become less tolerant of being told what to do. In both the Kroger and dcVAST stories, the company offered customers choices that allowed them to decide how they wanted the acquisition experience to unfold. In the case of the grocer, shoppers can choose to stand in line and have an employee scan and bag their purchases, or they can take over these tasks themselves and save time. dcVAST helps customers streamline the acquisition process regardless of who is delivering the service. So customers can elect to stay with the manufacturer if they choose, hire dcVAST, or arrange a combination of the two. The choice is theirs.

When examining the events surrounding the acquisition of your own offerings, you need to carefully identify sacrifices customers might encounter, such as an out-of-reach product, and work to eliminate them whenever you can. There is always a way to make the process better for the customer if you're creative and look at this stage through his eyes. This might mean making difficult decisions at times. If there's a bottle-neck in your distribution channel and your product isn't available when it should be, maybe you need a new distributor. If a retail environment makes it difficult or unpleasant to acquire your product, then perhaps you need to offer the customer alternatives, including Internet shopping. Delivering a friendlier buying experience may be as simple as training and empowering personnel to be more customer-focused. We'll talk about these issues in more detail in the next section. For now, the point is to *make it easy and pleasant* for people to buy your goods and services; otherwise they'll never make it to the next stage, and the Value Experience will be dead in its tracks.

Stage Four—Integrate

CONGRATULATIONS, customer and company have made it to the next level. Your offering has been purchased and now it's time for consumers to integrate their purchase into their lives. By definition, integration is the process of making something a part of the whole. This process can be simple or complex. If you purchase a carton of milk, for instance, the integration process would consist of putting the milk in your car, taking it home, and placing it in the refrigerator. Later you would open the carton, pour the milk into a glass, and eventually dispose of the empty carton. These events—carrying, storing, opening, and disposing—are all components of the experience of milk consumption. Every product has similar events, some more complex than others depending on the product. The number and complexity of events in this stage can have a serious impact on a Value Experience. For instance, as we saw in chapter 2, installation of a new computer takes place only once, but it can color the way you feel about computers for a very long time. One bad experience and you may never buy another PC. Toothpaste, on the other hand, isn't at all complex, but it's used twice a day. As long as applying and using the toothpaste goes smoothly, you'll probably buy the same brand again next time. But if the top always gets clogged or it doesn't foam right or taste good, a hundred or so repetitions of the event will have the same impact as a poor installation event. You won't be a repeat customer. So, as with every stage, if a business can identify a sacrifice and turn it into a reward, everyone benefits.

Have Milk, Will Travel

Let's look at milk again. Nearly every household in America has a carton of milk in the refrigerator; over 80 percent of all milk has been traditionally consumed at home. The problem, milk producers found, was that people were spending less and less time eating at home, and milk consumption was going down. In 1994 the average American consumed 585.8 pounds of dairy a year, but in 1996 that figure dropped to 575.6 pounds, according to U.S. Department of Agriculture figures.[20] In 1998, however, the tide began to turn—at least in some areas of the country. The reason for this unexpected surge in milk consumption wasn't due to a newfound love of milk. Americans have always liked dairy products. No, the reason for a 269 percent increase in milk sales in the Chicago market alone was the introduction of Milk Chug.[21] The brainchild of dairy leader Dean Foods, the new product makes milk a portable and convenient beverage at work, in the car, or anywhere one might drink a soda or a bottle of water.

The secret to Milk Chug's success is its packaging. Fashioned to look like the milk bottles once delivered to the home, but with resealable, screw-on caps, these easy-to-handle, brightly colored plastic containers come in pint, quart, and single-serve eight-ounce multipacks. Now people can find Milk Chug everywhere they'd normally stop for a can of soda, so they have a choice between more traditional on-the-go drinks or a healthy slug of milk. It's clear many are choosing the latter. Following the introduction of Milk Chug, the industry experienced its first per capita increase in milk consumption in more than twenty years.[22]

By recognizing the need its customers had for a more portable product, Dean Foods not only revitalized a mature market, it also provided its customers with a much richer integration experience. The easy-to-carry, easy-to-drink, and easy-to-dispose-of bottles were made to order for a Value Experience. In this case, Dean Foods met the challenge that all businesses face—keeping up with the evolving lifestyle needs of their Value Groups and changing or improving how products integrate into customers' lives accordingly. In the next section, we'll take a closer look at product and packaging design as a function of experience, but for now, let's look at how the integration stage works in the world of service.

While it is easy to think of goods in terms of integration because we purchase and then use them, we don't often think of services in the same way. But services, too, are subject to this stage. After all, everyone who buys a service has to take delivery of the service in some way—that's integration. Remember Tony, the guy in need of a good haircut? His integration stage began as soon as he arrived at the salon. There he had a check-in experience, a waiting experience, a shampoo and haircut experience, and a paying experience. We already know that not everything went as smoothly as he hoped. Tony had a busy schedule, so asking him to sacrifice time was not acceptable. Many service delivery situations are fraught with such pitfalls. Often process-driven, services today can be more about completing a process as quickly as possible than about taking care of customers, as the word "service" implies. But they don't have to be.

Getting Personal with Service

Marriott International has been serving busy travelers well for decades. In 1999 it won half of all of the J.D. Powers and Associates awards for the hotel industry and its occupancy rates have been consistently ten percentage points above the industry average.[23] The reason for both feats stems from meticulous attention to the delivery of service and consideration of the context of the customer experience. At several of its large resorts, for example, Marriott offers a number of activities and restaurants that appeal to vacationing guests. To make using these amenities easier, the hotel offers a "Personal Planning Service" that allows

Marriott to create custom itineraries. Once a reservation is made, a vacation planner uses information provided by the customer and preferences on file with the hotel to prepare for the ideal holiday. When the customer arrives, sometimes weeks later, tee times have been scheduled, dinner reservations arranged, sightseeing and recreation itineraries already planned. The hotel has made it easier to use the full range of its services; consequently, customers integrate these services into their vacation more often. Marriott has found that guests who participate in this program show noticeably higher guest satisfaction scores and spend an average of $100 more a day on services beyond the room rate. Guests also tend to return more often because Marriott has provided them with a great vacation experience.[24]

What is interesting about this story is the fact that the hotel employs the customer in creating a valuable integration experience. By asking in advance how the customer wants his vacation to unfold, the hotel can better control the rewards and sacrifices along the way. So instead of spending time making reservations and planning activities at the last minute (both time-wasting sacrifices), guests are relaxing and having fun. Only the customer can truly know how a product or service will best fit into his or her life and lead to a Value Experience. So the more you ask questions, solicit customer participation, and observe reactions, the better prepared you will be to deliver the experience your customers expect.

It's also a good idea to be your own customer whenever possible. How does your product or service stack up to your expectations as a consumer? What challenges do you encounter when you try to transport, use, store, or dispose of your product? What annoyances confront you as you receive, pay for, or report problems with your services? All of these events are part of the integration stage, and any one of them can win loyalty or cause defection. When there are too many sacrifices and not enough rewards, we already know what happens. Thus, it's critical to examine every event your customers experience while integrating your offering into their lives, whether this takes place at work or home. You may have succeeded brilliantly in the first three stages of the Experience Engagement Process and made the sale, but if you fall short here, the trip is over—that is, unless they have some reason to give you a second chance.

Stage Five—Extend

O NCE A CUSTOMER has purchased and used a product or service, what then? She can repurchase, setting in motion the acquire and integrate stages once again, or the experience can evolve into a relationship. This is the stage where company and customer form a bond beyond mere ownership or use of a product or service. It is where business reaches for the soul of the consumer.[25]

Consumers today are very complex. They often have a clearly defined social conscience; they are both emotional and informed, and while they do still make rational decisions, logic doesn't always rule the day.[26] Whenever a company can tap into the emotional or spiritual level of a person, it has a better chance of enhancing its value in that customer's eyes. Let's say, for example, a customer has a diabetic child. Product A is good, but product B donates part of its proceeds to the American Diabetes Association, so the customer buys product B. Even if product A is improved, chances are the customer still won't defect, staying instead with the company that has formed the emotional bond. The best way to develop a lasting relationship like this with your customers is by relating to their values and supporting what is important in their lives. One company that has done a remarkable job of aligning with its customers' values and turning that alignment into loyalty is Campbell Soup.

Labels and Loyalty

Since its founding more than one hundred years ago, the Campbell Soup Company has stood for wholesome nutrition and family values. In its advertising, promotional materials, and sponsorships, family and children have been a consistent and easily recognizable theme. Much to its credit, however, the company doesn't just give lip service to kids and families, it actively supports them. Since 1973, eighty thousand schools and organizations have received almost $100 million in free educational equipment through Campbell's Labels for Education (LFE) program. This program, which serves 50 million kids, allows customers to support their local schools by collecting labels from designated Campbell products. The school can then redeem the labels for computers, software, sports equipment, musical instruments, and even fifteen-passenger vans. Because of LFE, education and enrichment opportunities that might otherwise be lost to budget cuts remain a part of the students' lives. The initiative has been so successful that many schools have been participants for twenty years or more.[27]

Campbell's LFE program has also reaped rewards for the company by fostering amazing commitment and loyalty to the soup giant, at both the community and consumer level. In an interview with the company we learned that over one-third of American households with kids aged six to twelve participate in Campbell's LFE program. We also learned that these households purchase 44 percent more Campbell's soup than households that do not participate. National and local publicity on the program generated more than 77 million media impressions in 2001 alone, and consumer awareness of the program is at 67 percent. Most telling perhaps, is that fact that in 2001 alone, more than 300 *million* labels were redeemed. With this kind of recognition and participation, it is easy to see why competitors have been unable to unseat Campbell from its leadership position in the soup category, even though at times it has fallen behind in product innovation. People are willing to give the company a chance to catch up because doing business with Campbell Soup is not just about what's in the can.[28]

Bringing People Together

Another way to extend relationships with your customers is to form partnerships with them. Since Steelcase's primary business focus is the manufacture and service of products for workplace environments, the company hopes its customers will think of Steelcase whenever they need to create new space, renovate, move, merge, or simply add equipment. But, as we know, a company can never predict when a competitor might have an opportunity to move in. Perhaps a new facilities manager with loyalties to another company is hired. New budget directives may call for competitive bids, or a problem with a dealer might attach itself to the manufacturer. One way to ensure against such events, however, is through partnership.

For many companies, asset management is a tedious and expensive task, especially for items such as furniture. To help customers maintain better control over this cumbersome process, Steelcase developed the Furniture Management Coalition (FMC). This business partnership between Steelcase, a network of service providers, and the customer allows facilities managers to reduce costs, use their human resources more efficiently, procure equipment, and even dispose of furniture assets with greater ease. One FMC participant with more than fifteen thousand locations was able to reduce furniture services spending from approximately $13 million a year to $5 million in just three years. Another nine-state regional partner with over eight thousand locations maintained sixty-one warehouses at a cost of $1.1 million annually. In two years, FMC helped it reduce the number of warehouse locations from sixty-one to five, trimming annual costs to $216,000. A third national partner was able to reduce work order costs. The cost of moving people went from $200 down to $92 per work order. Maintenance costs fell from $90 to $72 per work order.[29] This type of customer-focused relationship is hard for companies to walk away from, and everybody wins.

Extension can also be achieved through facilitation. We mentioned earlier that Pharmacia's Rogaine Web site features chat rooms where people can talk to each other about hair loss treatment and concerns. With this feature customers can turn to Pharmacia not only to gain information that satisfies an intellectual need, but also to give and receive support, which adds a powerful emotional dimension. Although Pharmacia isn't directly involved in the chat, it facilitates an online community, which in turn adds value to the customer's relationship with the company.

Facilitation is also effective in bringing education to consumers. Purina Mills, now owned by Land O' Lakes, did extensive research on what suburban customers wanted. The company learned that educational programs that supported this market's lifestyle were highly valued. So in each of its America's Country Store retail outlets, Purina included features to help dealers facilitate education in the community.[30] Neighborhood bulletin boards, meeting space for local clubs, and weekend seminars with local experts on topics such as puppy training, buying your first horse, and pond maintenance bring great value to the consumer. This value is realized in several ways—as knowledge that helps people maintain and enhance their lifestyles, a feeling of belonging to a group of people with shared interests, and the sense that Purina cares about what's important to them.

By relating to your customers' values as Purina Mills, Campbell Soup, Pharmacia, and Steelcase have done, you gain a more intimate understanding of what is significant in their lives. With this insight you increase your chances of delivering what customers really want and you protect your business as well. In the final analysis, companies that have made an effort to move beyond the scope of their product to build relationships with their customers are more successful than those that don't.[31] It's as simple as that.

Full Circle

THE PURPOSE of this journey was to see the consumption experience through the customer's eyes. Standing on the company side, we often forget or are unaware of the impact our actions have on the people who keep us in business. If we want to succeed in the future, however, we have to take the blinders off. It's not enough to focus only on your product, because product is only one part of the customer experience, and as participants in that experience you are a part of every event.

From the moment customers have an impulse to purchase, you have an opportunity to help them discover the value you offer. During the evaluate stage you can help them make the right buying decision, one that will support their values and fit their situation. When you succeed and your goods or services are chosen, there are many ways to make acquiring them a satisfactory experience. Moreover, there are many opportunities to delight customers as they integrate products and services into their lives and even beyond as you work to build a lasting relationship.

It's true you may not be able to control every event along the way, but being aware of the possibilities can certainly help you minimize sacrifices while making the most of the experiences you can control. Once this customer understanding is within reach, you can turn your focus inward, as we're about to do. In the next part we'll look at the company's role in the Value Experience.

PRICELESS ROADMAP—CHAPTER 3

➤ Identify the events that occur during each stage of the Experience Engagement Process for your product or service.

➤ For each of your Value Groups, determine if these events are a reward, sacrifice, or neutral.

➤ Identify two or three opportunities to increase a reward, eliminate a sacrifice, or remove a neutral event within each stage.

➤ For each stage in the Experience Engagement Process, identify whether the customer is interacting with your product, service, or retail environment.

Creating Value through Experience

onday afternoon is quiet at Oak Brook Center. With Christmas just past, the Illinois weather is typically cold, keeping people away from the open-air shopping mall. The one exception is an unusual store with the intriguing name of Build-A-Bear Workshop. From the moment she walked through the brightly colored door, Diana knew that on this experience field trip, she was about to witness something priceless.[1]

Inside, a dozen or so children are bustling around the shop. They aren't sorting through piles of prefabricated stuffed animals as they might in other stores; they are busy at work creating their own. Diana sees two young girls with their dad, introduces herself, and asks if she can tag along as an observer. The parent agrees as Kris, who is eight, and Candice, who just turned five, hurry their father along to a row of barrels sitting kid-height on the floor. In each container is a supply of limp animal shells, waiting to be chosen as a lifelong friend of some eager child. The girls each choose a shell—Kris a polar bear and Candice a monkey. Then, fidgety and excited, they join the other children in line.

Before long the sisters are standing in front of the stuffing machine, a bright yellow contraption resembling a giant popcorn popper. Churning with polyester fill, it is attended by a Master Bear Builder who asks the children their names and gently explains the procedure. Normally this is done one child at a time, but the girls clearly want to stick together. First one then the other helps add fill to each animal by pressing on a floor pedal. As the creatures begin to take shape, a sound disk that will announce "I love you" every time a paw is pressed is inserted deep in the stuffing and more fill is added. Then it's time for a huggability test—and a bit of magic.

"This is your bear's heart," the Master Bear Builder tells them, handing each girl a tiny heart-shaped pillow made of red satin. "Now close your hands over it and make it real warm, like this." Demonstrating, she encourages them to do the same. "Okay now, blow into your hands and make a wish." Each child does as she's asked, eyes closed tightly as the wish is formed and transferred to the heart. Giggling when they're congratulated on doing it exactly right, they hand the precious objects over to be sealed inside.

The final task is to place a bar code in the bears to track them if they're ever lost and returned to the store. While this is being done and the last stitching is completed, Kris and Candice decide on names for their new friends: Rainbow and Willie. Finally holding their precious friends in their arms, Candice listens intently to hers and whispers, "Krissy, I can hear her heart."

If Maxine Clark, founder and "Chief Executive Bear" of the St. Louis–based company had been standing next to Diana as she witnessed this moment, there's no doubt she would have said that the wide-eyed wonder and the memories this experience creates for families are exactly why she started Build-A-Bear Workshop. It all began in 1996 when Maxine was looking for something new to do. After three and a half years as president of Payless ShoeSource, where she opened nearly a store a day for the $2.5 billion chain, the job became more about meetings and less about creativity. "My financial bank account was incredibly high," she says. "I worked so hard, I never had time to spend it. But my psychic bank account was empty."[2] While helping a friend chaperone a third-grade field trip to a toy factory, it began to fill up.

"The kids were asking a million questions," she recalls. "You could see that they were engaged with the novelty of learning something."[3] It was something Maxine never forgot—in fact, it was something she wanted to duplicate. So, idea in hand (or perhaps in heart), she set out to create a company that would inspire feelings of wonder and accomplishment in every child and adult who walked through the door.

This focus is one of the reasons why Build-A-Bear works so well. Everything about the company—all the various experience events it sets in motion—are directed by one central theme: to provide a fun and creative experience. That's why customers like Kris and Candice are never just waiting in line. Each step takes them closer to creating a singular friend. From strategically placed displays of clothing and accessories that allow builders to preplan what outfits their new buddies will wear to the computers where their creations are registered, everything inside the store is carefully orchestrated to support the intended theme.

Once the workshop adventure is completed, a newsletter and Web site extend the experience by offering tips on clothing and accessories. E-mails and letters also encourage kids to share creative ideas. Clark is especially sensitive to customer input. Early on, she established a Cub Advisory board made up of twenty children ranging in age from six to fourteen, and each night she answers e-mail from kids of all ages who create new friends in her workshops.

Encouraging this type of interaction and believing in the customers' ability to help make each experience a good one is something most companies fall short on. Several copycats have already cropped up and gone by the wayside, learning the hard way that the concept takes more than fluffy fill and acrylic skins. That Clark understands what it takes is evident in the astounding growth her company has experienced. Just three years after the first shop opened to rave reviews in the upscale St. Louis Galleria, the rapidly expanding stuffed animal chain topped $50 million in sales from thirty-nine stores. An additional thirty locations were planned for 2001. If it maintains its per-store sales average of $700 per square foot—more than double that of the average toy and hobby store—the company will undoubtedly be hailed as one of retail's most successful innovators.[4]

We already believe it is, not because the idea is so unique, but because the experience is so complete. If you look closely at Build-A-Bear you will find that the company has carefully controlled three key components critical to delivering a complete Value Experience. These magic ingredients are (1) product, which is any good, service, or family of products offered in the marketplace; (2) service, which encompasses all interactions between a company, its representatives, and the customer, such as customer service or repair service; and (3) environment, which deals with the external elements surrounding a product, such as packaging or marketplace. The company then provides a focus for all three components by creating an experience theme—in Build-A-Bear Workshop's case it's fun and creativity.

Every experience the company controls, no matter how mundane, is carefully planned to be fun and to foster imagination. For instance, checking out isn't usually an experience people look forward to. At Build-A-Bear, however, customers aren't just paying but continuing an experience. In addition to being the payment station, checkout is where customers receive their new toy's birth certificate and "bear condo," a distinctive house-shaped carrying box. On the Web site kids can literally dress their new friends online by calling up the appropriate animal image and selecting clothing and accessories. After a brief wait, the creature appears on screen wearing its new outfit. It's virtual dress-up. Whether a parent later buys or not, it's a fun, creative extension of the original experience. By creating a theme to link experience events, a company can not only guide a Value Experience, it can also replicate such events over and over again. Just as important, with a theme, a business can direct decisions about product, service, and environment to ensure each component adds to the value a company wants to deliver. Throughout this section, we'll see that when this happens within each component, the results are often astonishing.

As you read, keep in mind that our purpose in these chapters is to provide a *customer-centric* view focused solely on how a component impacts the Value Experience. For example, when we discuss product, we look at physical attributes, not from an engineering standpoint, but how factors such as color or the feel of a material contribute to the overall experience. Regarding environment, we look at how easy it is to open or dispose of packaging, not how well it fits on a store shelf. We can't possibly touch on every aspect of product, service, and environment in a single chapter (each component is worthy of its own book); we only want to start you thinking in the right direction—a direction that focuses first and foremost on the customer, the final ingredient in your success.

four

Getting a Grip

THE PRODUCT COMPONENT

A S SAM FARBER WATCHED HIS WIFE PEELING APPLES for a tart he couldn't help but notice her wincing in pain. An arthritis sufferer, even a simple task like gripping a kitchen utensil caused her discomfort, but she loved cooking so she suffered through it. Farber understood. He shared her culinary passion and knew what she'd be sacrificing if she had to give up cooking. Before that happened, however, he was determined to do something to help. The question was what.[1]

Over the next few weeks, Farber, the retired CEO of housewares manufacturer Copco, considered the problem. He himself had often found kitchen utensils uncomfortable to use. Recognizing that most of the shortcomings stemmed from design, he called Davin Stowell, founder of Smart Design, a product development firm. They talked for hours about the gross inadequacies of everyday cooking tools and how they could be improved. Before long they decided the only solution was to scrap traditional models and start over. Working from the concept of Universal Design, which focuses on the comfort and ease of users, they tackled the peeler first.

Anytime someone picks up a peeler to skin a fruit or vegetable, several dynamics are set in motion. The palm and fingers have to grip, the wrist has to turn and twist, and even the elbow gets in on the action. So in order to create a peeler that was easy and comfortable to use, the design team analyzed the motion and amount of pressure needed to accomplish the task. Their findings were then translated into design elements, each focused on one common goal—to make peeling trouble-free. Working through scores of Styrofoam and wood mock-ups, they finally succeeded, and the OXO Good Grips Swivel Peeler was born. From feel to function, it was exactly what they had envisioned. Anyone, even Farber's wife, could use it with ease. The new peeler was an instant hit, winning numerous design awards. Today it is on permanent display at the Museum of Modern Art in New York.

From this initial success OXO went on to develop more than 350 Good Grips utensils. Profitable in its first full year of operation, sales continued to grow at a rate of 50 percent a year. OXO today claims 15 percent of the market, despite the fact that its products cost up to three times as much as the grocery store variety. KitchenAid, Oneida, and Farberware are all attempting to copy the look and feel of OXO's products, but there is still nothing quite like Farber's creations.

What sets OXO and Good Grips apart is the fact that Farber and company weren't just selling kitchen utensils. They offered a more efficient and comfortable experience in the kitchen—an experience every cook, arthritic or not, immediately values. This is the role products play in the Value Experience—to provide form, function, and design that support or enhance a customer's life.[2] For many involved in product and service design, this definition is a departure from traditional thinking. Most of us are used to looking at goods and services for what they do, rather than how they affect the customer. If we want to deliver a Value Experience, however, the old perspective won't work. The customer must always remain in view if we want to succeed. To that end, as we explore the various aspects of products and services in this chapter, we'll focus only on those characteristics that specifically impact experience. Our examination will involve four specific areas. These are *physical attributes,* or the characteristics of the various parts that make up a product. *Process attributes* are much like their physical counterparts, but apply solely to service products. *Aesthetic attributes* relate to the way in which a product impacts our senses, and *associative attributes* refer to branding, endorsements, awards, and so forth. Each of these elements plays a critical role in determining what the customer thinks and feels and ultimately what kind of value he or she receives from a product.

As in previous chapters, we'll look at specific offerings that deliver value to customers and profits to their companies. They should start you thinking about your own goods and services and how looking at them in a new light—one that shines from the customer side of the aisle—can help revitalize sagging brands, energize a mature company, or bring innovations to the market that really are truly original.

Let's Get Physical

E VERY MANUFACTURED GOOD is made up of parts, each having physical attributes that together define the product. For instance, a pencil can be described by its attributes as being a wood casing six inches long with a core of #2 lead and a .5 mm rubber eraser at one end. Three parts—wood casing, graphite core, and eraser—each possessing specific characteristics. In terms of experience, however, physical attributes not only define a product; they also play a significant role in the experience a product delivers. Let's look at our pencil again. As it was described, this pencil can be comfortably held in an adult's hand (six inches long). It allows the user to write with minimal friction (a characteristic of #2 lead) and eradicate mistakes without changing instruments (thanks to the eraser). All in all, a satisfactory pencil-writing experience. But what if instead of being six inches long, the pencil were two inches long? It would still be a pencil, still write without friction, and still erase, but an adult would have a much more difficult time using it. This would not be a satisfactory writing experience. So different attributes create different experiences.

For a product to contribute to a Value Experience, its physical attributes must support, or at least not detract from, the overall value. This is true if a product has one part or tens, hundreds, even thousands of parts. Since we're familiar with the OXO Good Grips Swivel Peeler, we'll use it to examine how physical attributes contribute to an exceptional experience.

Coming to Grips with Design

From the beginning, Sam Farber and Smart Design set out to create a new utensil that was comfortable, effective, and required as little pressure and motion as possible to complete its task. If they were successful, anyone would be able to use the utensil. So with a theme of comfort and ease of use in mind, they began looking at the parts necessary to deliver the desired experience, beginning with the handle.

Most kitchen utensils have handles that are small in diameter and made of hard plastic. To make their peeler more comfortable, the designers envisioned a wider handle that fit more naturally in the palm of the hand. This change helped, but the peeler still wasn't as comfortable as they hoped. Hundreds of mock-ups later, Farber finally zeroed in on the problem. "Why can't we create a handle with a soft, squishy feel? One that invites you to grab it."[3] The designers agreed it was a good idea, but what material could provide this kind of comfort and still be durable enough to be used on a handle? Surprisingly, the answer came from a dishwasher gasket.

After researching a variety of materials, Smart Design discovered Santoprene®, a processed rubber with the soft feel Farber envisioned. Now all they needed was "squishy." Santoprene came to the rescue for this as well when, in a departure from traditional handle design, engineers used the material to create a series of flexible "fins," or small flaps, that compress slightly when pressure is applied. These fins worked especially well for the fingerprint hot spots—the places on the handle where the thumb and index finger grip. This was the "squish" Farber was looking for; it not only felt good, but also helped reduce stress on the hand. OXO had its good grip.

Next designers turned to the blade. Dissecting the action of peeling, they determined that if the blade swiveled, the person doing the peeling didn't have to twist her wrist. This eliminated a potentially painful motion. They also found that if the utensil was especially sharp, it cut down on the amount of pressure one had to apply. The designers enlisted the help of a group of engineers who had earned their reputation producing samurai swords and put them to work on the peeler blade. In short order, the engineers came up with a cutting edge that was razor-sharp and so thin it removed only the skin of the fruit or vegetable, not chunks of produce as other peelers often did. With the blade issue resolved, they then created a raised, curved blade shield to protect users from the sharp cutting edge while still allowing easy cleaning, whether by hand or in the dishwasher. With this final piece in place, all of the parts, the handle, the blade, and the shield, worked in harmony to create the intended experience—an easy, comfortable way to peel fruits and vegetables (see table 4-1).

TABLE 4 - 1

OXO Good Grips Swivel Peeler

Experience Objective	Physical Attribute	Experience Delivered
Comfortable to use with reduced stress on hand and wrist	Large diameter handle	Fits in palm, doesn't require fingers to close tightly
	Flexible fins	Reduced pressure at gripping points, squishy feel
	Pivoting blade	Requires no twisting of wrist when peeling
	Santoprene grip	Softer than plastic
Precision peeling	Pivoting blade	Smooth, clean action
	Razor-sharp, .8 to 1 mm stainless steel blade	Removes only skin
Easy to clean	Raised blade guard	Blade cleans easily
	Santoprene grip	Dishwasher safe
	Flexible fins	Small particles can't lodge in fins
Safe	Raised blade guard	Protects user from blade
	Santoprene grip	Doesn't get slippery when wet

Farber's peeler serves as an excellent example of what can be done when product development begins with the customer experience in mind. Good Grips was created for the comfort of the consumer, and that ultimately is what set it apart from the competition. If a product hasn't been consciously designed to deliver a specific experience, that doesn't mean it's doomed, however. Most products in existence today weren't designed with a definite experience in mind. When this is the case, you don't necessarily have to go back to the drawing board, but you do need to know exactly what experiences you're delivering. Then as the opportunity presents itself for improvement, you know where to focus.

For several decades, the mantra of the product development team has been features and benefits, not experiences. To some this might seem a fine distinction, because we equate benefits with value. The traditional look at features and benefits, however, concerns itself with an engineering-driven, rational, and analytical view of the parts of a product and how each of those parts performs a task. Experience, on the other hand, is holistic. When looking at product features and benefits from an experiential point of view we can't just look at specific functions of a product and what that isolated feature delivers, we also have to consider how those functions together impact the customer. In other words, we need to expand the definition of features and benefits to include the actual customer experience. The peeler isn't just a handle, blade, and blade shield; it's a peeling experience that is made better or worse by the physical attributes of its parts. This is an important distinction. Since this concept can be a bit confusing, let's look at another product that is more complex and even has a few flaws.

Almost Perfect

The Cuisinart cordless rechargeable hand blender can be used to blend drinks or chop small amounts of food. Although we generally like Cuisinart products, this one leaves us with mixed feelings, especially if, as we believe, the company's goal was to deliver a "comfortable and convenient" cordless food preparation experience. Physically, the blender is eighteen inches long and built in three removable sections. The first section consists of a nine-inch shaft containing the blade. When removed from the rest of the appliance, it can be rinsed in the sink or thrown in the dishwasher without getting the electrical parts wet. The blade also pops out easily for changing or cleaning.

The second section contains the battery. For those of us who have more battery chargers than we know what to do with stuffed in some obscure drawer, the Cuisinart approach to recharging the battery is refreshing and unique. After removing the battery section, you push on a small lever and an AC connector pops out of the side of the product. The battery section can then be plugged into an outlet and soon you're ready to go.

Storing the blender has been clearly thought out as well. The base is constructed in two pieces so that you can leave the pieces together for shelf storage or separate them to mount the blender on the wall (screws included), where it can hang within easy reach. Other features we found interesting were the alignment of the on-off switch with natural hand position and a snap ring collar for switching blades easily. We did find, however, that the hand blender is a bit oversized and heavy for use by a shorter woman working at countertop height. So as good as the product is, it does have an Achilles heel. It's uncomfortable for shorter customers who have to use the appliance with a raised arm.

Engineers might argue that the size and weight, which result from the motor and battery selection, are necessary if the Cuisinart is going to crush ice or blend twenty drinks without recharging. If that's the case, then in order to have a smaller and lighter product you would have to give up battery life and power. The question then becomes, Which is more important? The only way for Cuisinart to answer that question is to ask its Value Groups. Since many refrigerators offer crushed-ice makers, the heavy motor needed for that task might not be necessary. Or marketing might find that weight is only an issue for one Value Group—those using the product for cooking (which may often be women) versus those keeping the blender on hand to make drinks in the bar area. In either case, marketing would have greater insight into customer needs and engineering would have a better understanding of the consequences of its battery and motor choice. If both departments remain focused on the customer experience in this way, the company should be able to create a more elegant, experience-friendly design. In the long run their efforts could mean substantial revenue for the company.

In 1999 *BusinessWeek* sponsored the "Designs of the Decade: Best in Business 1990–1999 Awards" competition. For the first time in any formal competition, companies were required to show in quantitative terms the impact design had on a company's bottom line. Criteria included measurements such as market share, brand strength, and corporate image. They also evaluated financial performance in terms of annual growth in profits, margins, and stock price, return on investment, and major cost savings. Entrants then had to show a direct correlation between the various benchmarks and product design.[4] It's not surprising that the winners were products we're very familiar with, such as Apple's iMac and OXO Good Grips. What we found interesting about them, however, is the fact that in nearly every case, engineering, marketing, manufacturing, and service all worked together to deliver an exceptional experience.[5]

When reviewing your own products, search for ways to improve the value you deliver and/or eliminate product characteristics that detract from the desired experience. Negative attributes create sacrifices that may undermine the Value Experience. (The heavy, ice-crushing Cuisinart motor could fall into this category.)

Also look for physical attributes that aren't necessarily sacrifices but don't support your experience goals. If they're not bringing value to the customer, they are probably neutral and may be adding cost without benefit. When you look at every part of your product to determine its role in the overall experience, you can make more informed decisions about product design and refinement. You will also be better prepared to deal with the inherent trade-offs that occur in any design process, such as cost versus benefit, making it easier to know where to invest money and where to cut expenses. In the end, you'll have a product with purpose and a company with profits—something every company strives for.

Serving up a Value Experience

S O FAR we've said that manufactured goods and services are essentially the same when viewed in terms of value. As we examine product attributes, however, we need to make a distinction in vocabulary between the two. While goods have physical parts, services have process elements. Like physical attributes, these elements also have quantifiable characteristics that define and differentiate the service and directly affect the value of the experience. For instance, using waiters to serve customers is an expected element of a fine restaurant. The *number* of waiters working a particular shift, however, would be a characteristic of that restaurant's offering and therefore would directly affect the quality of the experience. Let's say in restaurant A, three waiters are employed to cover eighteen tables, and in restaurant B, three waiters cover only twelve tables. The customers at restaurant B would have more attentive service. So while the diners in the first restaurant might have an ordinary dining experience, those in the second one might have an extraordinary event.

Of course, other elements of the restaurant's process, such as reservations, parking, and paying the bill, will also impact the customer's experience. It is the combination of all these attributes that creates the overall value. However, individual attributes can act as differentiators, just as exceptional physical attributes can set one manufactured good apart from another. We'll compare two companies with common elements, but very different process attributes. At the end of the example, you decide which one you would rather do business with.

Service with Dispatch

Our two companies are dispatch centers. The first center averages eight staffers answering the phones every shift, with each call taking approximately five minutes to process. Using this ratio, each dispatcher can theoretically handle twelve calls an hour, for a total of ninety-six calls throughout the center. This number of calls, by the way, is exactly what the call center averages during off-peak hours. To some, this level of staffing might seem efficient—having only the number of people you need to take the calls during slow times. Unfortunately, customers don't cooperate by calling exactly every five minutes and only during off-peak hours. Instead they call at random, so inevitably callers have the pleasure of listening to Muzak for five to fifteen minutes before talking to a warm body. During peak hours backup is even longer. If the wait is going to be longer than twenty minutes, a message tells the caller that all representatives are busy assisting other customers, so please call back.

Our next dispatch center takes the same number of calls, but has thirty people manning the phones. In addition, the company has newer software and better training, so its people can process a service request very quickly. This frees employees to focus on understanding the customer's situation. In addition, because the staff is well trained and not stressed by a growing backlog of calls, they tend to be more pleasant and professional when dealing with customers. If a customer is upset, they have the time and the composure to deal with the problem. In between calls, this center's staff keys in service data so files are always up to date.

In each case the elements—staffing, training, and systems that are common to many services—are the same, but the attributes are very different. Our first dispatch center uses outdated and cumbersome software and is understaffed. The second center offers better training, has efficient dispatch software, and is properly staffed to deliver the best customer experience. The bonus for the company is happy customers and high productivity. These two companies may be doing the same work, but with different process attributes, they are delivering a much different experience to the customer. Which would you rather do business with? Clearly the second.

So, just as product companies need to identify all their physical attributes and determine whether they enhance, undermine, or don't affect the perception of value, so should service companies evaluate their process attributes. When services are approached in this way, improvement in both the customer experience and the benefit to the company can be dramatic, as our next story shows.

The Coast Starlight

Once considered a luxury product, travel by train was exemplified by fine dining, impeccable service, men in suits, and ladies in hats and gloves. Over time, however, the standards changed. What was once the province of the rich is now viewed as a purely functional and utilitarian mode of transportation—a way to get from point A to point B. Amtrak is attempting to change this perception by focusing on the elements of the trip that turn simple transportation into a Value Experience.[6] To facilitate the transformation, it turned over key routes to line directors and let each of them imprint a personal stamp on its product.

Brian Rosenwald, general manager of the Coast Starlight, which runs from Los Angeles to Seattle, chose to create a cruise-like experience for his customers. Each event during the trip—from arriving at the train station with baggage in hand to dining, socializing, and turning in for the night—was carefully orchestrated to be as much an element of the vacation as the final destination. Here's how the company describes it:

The Coast Starlight is a progressive party that gets you together with a fun crowd and takes you to all the hot spots on the West Coast: Seattle, Portland, Eugene, San Francisco, Monterey, Santa Barbara and Los Angeles. En route the scenery creates a gorgeous backdrop—snow-covered mountains, dense forests, fertile valleys and long stretches of Pacific Ocean shoreline. Amtrak gets you in the mood with regional cuisine and local wines. There are plenty of places to stop along the way. Stroll along Cannery Row and Fisherman's Wharf. Take a break in Paso Robles where you can visit one of over 48 wineries or relax in the natural hot springs. Stop in San Luis Obispo, take a scenic tour along the Pacific Coast and climb the enchanted hill to Hearst Castle. Aboard The Coast Starlight, you're our special guest—nothing is too good for you![7]

To deliver on the last promise, Amtrak has outfitted the train with elegant dining cars; a fun lounge for snacks, drinks, and entertainment; a theatre car; a parlor; and a special area for kids. To accommodate outdoor enthusiasts, a significant Value Group for this line, the Coast Starlight also offers storage for surfboards, bikes, golf clubs, and skis. Equally accommodating is the service. From stewards in starched shirts to fresh flowers daily, attention to detail confirms that the staff is committed to delivering a first-class experience. Room calls are answered promptly, meals served with spirited flair, and beds turned down each night. At trip's end, sleeping-car passengers are presented with a gift of two wine flutes and a split of sparkling wine. Nice touch, and all part of the process to ensure the Coast Starlight is not just a train ride, but a Value Experience that guests will fondly remember. Fortunately, it seems to be working. Although Amtrak is still struggling financially, the efforts it's made to improve its offering did allow the company to achieve record revenue of $1.8 billion in 1999, with the number of riders increasing for thirteen consecutive quarters.

As you examine your service product, first determine what Value Experience you are trying to deliver; then fine-tune your process attributes to make sure each supports your theme. Be sure to set the proper service levels for each Value Group. For example, in chapter 3 we looked at dcVAST. Its employees evaluated a customer's service needs to determine which equipment was critical and needed the best service coverage and which equipment required only minimal coverage. The same principle applies here. If you deliver the right service in the right way, your customers will receive the value they deserve. Also look for elements that are contradictory or unrelated to what you are trying to deliver. Eliminating these characteristics will ensure that your service is a real Value Experience and not just something that looks pretty on the surface. However . . . there is something to be said for good looks.

Touch Me, Feel Me

TECHNICALLY speaking, our next product attribute—aesthetics— is physical in nature. But even though aesthetics is based on physical attributes, it is much more than the sum of its parts and delivers a special type of value deserving our attention. Imagine if you will a 1946 Wurlitzer jukebox nestled in the corner of a dimly lit room. Its lights are pulsing while bubbles wind up the multicolored tubes in the large glass front. Mesmerized, you watch a 78-RPM record magically rise and settle on the platter. The needle gently swings into place and then slowly descends onto the record. As the first notes escape from the fifty-year-old speakers the sound is less than perfect, but you don't care. It's no longer just music. Sight and sound combine to provide an experience that is sensuous, nostalgic, and so uniquely Wurlitzer that people are willing to pay as much as $10,000 to own one. Such is the power of the senses—sight, sound, touch, taste, and smell.[8] One or more can and should play an important role in your Value Experience because, as we know, customers don't just react to a product on one level, they experience it with body, mind, emotions, and spirit.

Sight

When you walk into the fresh produce department of a grocery store your eyes are treated to a landscape of color—bright oranges, vibrant Red Delicious apples, sunny yellow bananas, and fat purple grapes cascading over the edge of their bin. Everything looks perfect, and on closer examination every piece of fruit and every vegetable nearly is. In the produce business, great care is taken with appearance because grocers know that visual appeal sells their products. That's why some fruits are dyed to give them a brighter, more appealing color and others are waxed and polished before making an appearance. All this fuss to tantalize us into taking produce home—but it works.

Sight is one of the most powerful senses affecting consumption.[9] It helps us capture objective facts such as color, shape, and size and register impressions about physical characteristics, including volume, weight, and texture. What we see also allows us to register subjective reactions. The rich look of gold, the efficiency of steel, the sophistication of chrome—all of these interpretations stem from vision and form a part of the customer experience. For the most part, businesses are accustomed to using this sense to add appeal to products and services, but the visual experience can offer more—or less—value depending on how it's used.

The System Link universal remote manufactured by Thomson Consumer Electronics uses color, size, and button shape to make its product less confusing and therefore a better experience. As a universal remote, it controls several different systems such as the TV, VCR, and surround sound. Anyone who's used this type of remote knows how annoying it can be to find the right buttons for the right device. The System Link eliminates much of the guesswork by color-coding equipment-specific functions and making the more commonly used buttons on the remote, such as volume control and channel selection, more accessible by enlarging them. This simple visual enhancement puts this product heads above others on the market.

Mercedes-Benz used to do something similar with visual attributes, but sadly it discontinued the feature. In one of its older sedans, seat adjustment was made easier by placing a seat-shaped control on the door, just above the armrest. If you pushed back on the top of the control, the seat reclined. When you pushed down on the front, the leading edge of the seat lowered. For all of us who have pushed the seat control the wrong way and squashed our knees into the steering wheel, this "picto-control" was a nice touch, and one that didn't cost much more than a round or square control. This feature was a "what you see is what you get" element, which leads to a better experience. This is as true for services as it is for products.

For example, who would you trust more to do your tax returns, someone who presented your finished return with correction fluid dabbed throughout the document, or one who encased your correction-free papers in a professional folder, neatly organized and ready to process? Visual characteristics help set expectations, align your goods and services with the value you are trying to deliver, and add to that value by enriching the experience. People believe what they see with their own eyes, so make sure the visual message you're sending is the right one.

Touch

Like sight, touch also helps form impressions and opinions that translate into value.[10] The whisper-soft feel of a cashmere sweater slipping over your skin creates a wonderful physical sensation that makes you feel pampered and elegant. These physical and emotional reactions are accompanied by the intellectual certainty that a sensation this good must be expensive. By the same token, denim is rough and sturdy, a fabric that says "let's get our hands dirty" or "go out and play." How many of you begin to relax the instant you pull on a pair of jeans? Through the sense of touch we can deliver subtle messages about the value of a product, whether it is a solid feel that conveys a sense of durability; an effortless, fluid sensation that connotes precision engineering; or a silky, luxurious texture that connotes elegance.

Another good example is the OXO Good Grips Swivel Peeler with the fins made of Santoprene. These fins are now a distinctive trademark of the product line, but they almost didn't make it into production when one of the engineers suggested replacing them with a spongy part in the handle. Known for giving design engineers free rein, it was expected that Sam Farber would agree, but this time he didn't. Not only did the entrepreneur have a clear vision of what the product should be, he brought an astute understanding of consumers to the table. As designer Davin Stowell tells it, Farber drove home the point that when people touch the fins, they immediately know they are about to have a different food preparation experience.

> *Their hand picks up the handle; their fingers go to those fins and start playing with them. It registers in their minds that we're saying: This is a better grip. Many people overlook that psychological connection. They think, if we make it work better, we can leave it there, but you can't. You've got to make sure that your customer understands right away.*[11]

This same principle applies to all products. When picking up a DeWALT 14.4-volt cordless drill, the grip is comfortable and the product feels balanced, with equal weight in front of and behind your hand. It *feels* easy to handle, and you want people to realize that right in the store. We have a friend who bought a DeWALT 14.4-volt drill rather than the 12-volt model for just this reason. The 12-volt model, with a smaller and lighter battery, felt as though it was falling forward out of his hand.

This painted an undesirable mental picture of the experience he would have using the tool. In this case he bought a more expensive, better-designed product from the same company, but he could just as easily have purchased another brand, costing the company a sale. It isn't always good to reserve quality features, particularly those that convey subtle messages, only for the more expensive products. When you do, it leaves your lower price lines open for competitive assault, a circumstance that might be avoided by adding something as simple as better balance to a power tool. When you pay attention to these critical details, you can almost hear the door slamming in the competition's face.

Sound

When sound makes the *Wall Street Journal,* you know it's serious. In an article entitled "Acoustics Are the New Frontier in Designing Luxury Automobiles," they document the luxury automobile industry's quest for perfection in sound engineering.[12] The reason for this quest is twofold. First, companies such as BMW, Mercedes, Jaguar, Lincoln, and even Land Rover want to give customers a better experience and feeling of satisfaction—if it sounds well made, it probably is. Second, these companies hope to help distinguish themselves from other luxury models, which today look, act, and feel pretty much the same. So in places like Munich, Stuttgart, and Detroit, acoustic engineers listen to revving motors, idling blinkers, and the thownking of windshield wipers trying to determine the right sound signature for their brand. Mercedes, for instance, is going for traditional and conservative. BMW is pleased when an engine emits a sporty growl. "It's an art, deciding what the correct sound for each brand is," says Wolfgang Reitzle, the former number-two executive at BMW and now Ford's luxury-brand czar. "It's all about capturing the essence of the brand."[13]

Sometime the essence of the brand is best served by eliminating sound. No one really cares for the sound that windshield washers make, but eliminating it presented some unique challenges for BMW. Early on engineers were able to deaden the noise of the wiper motor with sound-absorbing padding, but the rubber blades still made a slapping sound at the top of their arc. After months of testing, they found that a hardening of the rubber blade as it sat unused was causing the noise. To remedy the problem they engineered a solution whereby every few days the wiper motors would automatically flip the resting position of the blades, keeping the rubber soft and, best of all, silent. They're still working on the blinkers. Gerhard Thoma, a BMW sound engineer, admits that no one will buy a car because they like the turn signal sound. "But it is all part of the impression that we want to make," he says. "It's the little things that count."[14] How true.

A few months ago we bought a replacement Hewlett-Packard printer for the office. There was nothing wrong with our older HP; we were just looking for higher print quality and faster printing. After setting up the new model, loading paper, and sending off our first document, we were dismayed to find that the printer sounded like it was eating itself alive. Each time a piece of paper loaded, a loud clanking erupted from beneath the plastic covers. This was not good. It really did sound like it was breaking.

Later, we went back to the store where we purchased it only to be told this noise was normal. We're not sure who decided this was normal, but we didn't like it and returned the printer. At the moment our old, reliable, and quiet printer is still in use, but when we do get around to replacing it, we'll at least look at other brands. When a company like Hewlett-Packard gets so many things right, it's shocking when a detraction this blatant gets through. We shouldn't have to make a printer-purchasing decision based on sound, but that particular noise told us that something was wrong with the product, even if officially it was "normal."

This ability to give voice to the value of your product is probably the most important role of sound. Through the sense of hearing, a product talks to the customer in a way no other senses can. In the case of luxury cars, it says you are part of a distinctive community—only a member of the "family" owns this sound. Other sounds convey a sense of security, like the satisfying click of a lock tumbling into place. Another, like the purr of the refrigerator or the famous Tupperware "burp," might say, "I'm working." Sound can heighten anticipation—for instance, the gurgling of a coffeemaker or the revving of a high-performance engine just before it kicks into an exhilarating burst of speed. What are you saying to your cus-tomers? Whether it's your product, your phone system, or the front door doing the talking, make sure it's sending the message you want to deliver.

Smell

From that new-car smell to the tantalizing aroma of simmering coffee beans, the sense of smell has a unique impact on the consumer. An aroma can make the mouth water or eyes tear. It can be sensuous or comforting. It can even resurrect memories—perhaps of a lost love, a favorite grandmother, or a scare in a dark cellar. Many industries recog-nize the power the nose can bring to an experience; that's why cleaning products smell like lemon or pine, why candles come in every fragrance found in nature and then some, and why real estate agents pop an apple pie in the oven on open-house day.

But what if aroma just isn't one of your product's qualities? Do you just skip it and go on? You could, but with a little imagination you might find a use for the nose after all. One computer service company had a reputation for doing excellent work. Unfortunately, since most of their work was done inside machines and often after hours, it was transpar-ent. After looking for a way to use the senses to enhance the customer experience, the company decided to wipe down each computer case with a fresh-smelling cleaner every time a service technician completed his or her work. Before long, customers began commenting on how well their systems were working after a service call. The work itself had not changed, but people associated the clean smell with renewal and order, much the same way one feels when a house has just been cleaned.

Just as adding smell can help a product, removing it can hurt. Envi-ronmentally friendly disks that wash loads of clothes without detergent were never able to get off the ground, primarily, it was found, because the disks didn't leave behind that clean-clothes smell. Maybe the man-ufacturer should have included scented dryer sheets with every product to get around the no-scent objection. This is where knowing your Value Groups can help. Is there a smell that your Value Groups associate with something important ? Odors associated with freshness, the outdoors, or even with certain occupations can enhance an experience. The Home

Depot keeps a sawdust smell in its stores to entice its predominately male customers. We swear one restaurant in the area deliberately vents its stoves to catch the north wind so the smell of grilling steaks tantalizes every passing car. And who hasn't been seduced by the scent of cinnamon in the mall or airport and found himself mysteriously standing in front of a Cinnabon counter? Scent is not for every product, but if you can find a way to incorporate it into the experience you deliver, it can add delightful value.

Taste

Taste is the most difficult sense to incorporate in an experience because if your product isn't meant to be put in the mouth, then of course taste doesn't apply. In fact, we thought about leaving it out. However, in the spirit of the experience adventure we decided to see if we could uncover ways to bring this discriminating sense into an overall company experience. To that end, we held a brainstorming session on this topic with a group of people from different departments in a client company. Although we have to admit this wasn't our most successful such gathering, it was certainly fun. Shipping wanted beer-flavored toothpicks with every carryout lunch order; sales just wanted the beer. Operations thought lemon-flavored water cups might be nice, and accounts payable suggested flavored glue on envelopes—maybe a fresh cinnamon taste to make paying bills more pleasant. Later we learned that mint-flavored envelopes are already available, but sadly not used for bills—at least not at this company. If they were, clearly the taste would have been remembered.

Making a favorable impression, being remembered, giving something of value to the customer that adds to her enjoyment, comfort, or emotional, intellectual, or spiritual well-being—these elements are what the Value Experience is all about. The senses provide endless opportunities to support and enhance the value we bring to customers if we take the time to explore the possibilities. Whether it is a shape that makes life easier, a feel that delights, a scent that brings back memories, or a taste that tantalizes, the senses can help build an association with value in a powerful and lasting way—and as we'll see, association has a power all its own.

The Company You Keep

W E'VE ALL HAD those moments when a well-known brand; a popular public figure; a situation, event, or even imagery has caused us to register ideas, feelings, sensations, or memories about a product or service. When this happens, we're tapping into the *associative attributes* of that product or service. Defined as the characteristics that attach themselves to an offering as a result of an outside influence, associative attributes can greatly impact a Value Experience. Let's say, for example, your father took you to Chicago Cubs baseball games as a child. Just the two of you would take off on a Saturday afternoon and sit in ivy-covered Wrigley Field eating hot dogs and cheering for the home team. On your tenth birthday, your dad buys you an official Cubs jacket and it becomes one of your most cherished possessions. It's true you like the Cubs, but a good part of the value of the garment is its association with the time you spent with your dad. The ability of the jacket to trigger a memory is that product's associative attribute.

This type of association, a common marketing strategy, is used most often to create an emotional bond with the consumer.[15] As part of the Value Experience, however, associations shouldn't just address emotions; they should also support the values you wish to represent. Golfer Tiger Woods, for example, has become well known not only for his exceptional perform-ance on the golf course, but also for his hard work and playful nature. These associative attributes have been put to good use by Buick, which has this to say about its relationship with Woods: "Golf is a sport of skill, patience, and perseverance—the same qualities we apply when it comes to building some of the world's finest vehicles."[16] By aligning itself with Woods, the company can communicate the desired workmanship message and at the same time make a very powerful value statement—if Tiger likes it, it must be wonderful because he doesn't have to settle for anything less.

We would take this association one step further. Far from being seen as "playful" or "fun-loving," Buick is generally associated with more mature drivers. But its alignment with the youthful, energetic Tiger is beginning to change that image, and for the first time in decades, the company can realistically hope a younger audience will discover how good its cars really are. This hope can be realized only if it can translate these associative attributes into physical attributes, such as a more contemporary design or features that cater to a more adventuresome driver. What these associations imply must match the value the product actually delivers. Without alignment of associative attributes and value, Buick just has another celebrity ad, not the makings of a Value Experience.

Association can also be achieved through more subtle means. The DeWALT power tools we mentioned earlier, for example, sport a bright yellow casing. This yellow is the same color used by Caterpillar on its three-ton articulated earthmover and is associated with rugged performance; thus, buyers transfer their beliefs about Caterpillar quality to DeWALT. Calphalon made its mark with professional-grade cookware designed to satisfy the most painstaking chefs but tough enough to stand up to the rigors of a busy kitchen. When it entered the home market, Calphalon brought with it an association with demanding five-star chefs. The fact that both products do indeed deliver performance and durability makes the association work as part of the Value Experience. Otherwise, these attributes are just marketing without meaning. When used properly, associations can communicate value in a very unique way.

Viewing your product or service as something that delivers and communicates value, rather than mere form or function, is an important step in integrating the ideals of the Value Experience into your company culture. If you use the Experience Engagement Process to uncover the various events surrounding your offering, you may find several ways to increase rewards and limit sacrifices through physical and process attributes, creative use of the senses, or by association. To do so, however, you must remember that from a value perspective, you are no longer selling remote controls or tax preparation, train rides or vegetable peelers. You are delivering and communicating an important *part* of a complete Value Experience. In its totality, your offering is much less vulnerable to assault, because it is no longer meeting the market on its own. As we examine the remaining components of the Value Experience, keep this in mind—with the support of service and environment, a product becomes greater than the sum of its parts and more valuable to customers and your company than you ever thought possible.

PRICELESS ROADMAP—CHAPTER 4

➤ Identify the physical, process, aesthetic, and associative attributes of your offering.

➤ For each attribute, identify whether it contributes to the experience objective, detracts from it, or has no impact.

➤ For each attribute, identify opportunities to enhance the Value Experience you deliver.

Was It Good for You, Too?

THE SERVICE COMPONENT

I T'S 2:30 IN THE MORNING AT A PETROCHEMICAL plant on the Houston Ship Channel. While everyone sleeps, a monitor in the electrical substation records a major power surge and kills the utility feed. Automatically a backup generator kicks in, but not before several drives are damaged. Within minutes a Web server in the industrial controller senses the damage and begins broadcasting alerts. The first e-mail goes to the plant manager's wireless phone. The second is sent to the company's electrical contractor, Square D. A final e-mail goes to the manufacturer of the damaged drives, putting in a rush order for replacements.

By the time the plant manager arrives at 6:30 A.M., Square D is already installing the new drives and one of its engineers is on the phone. She's analyzed the incident data and found a pattern of erratic power. After talking with the plant manager, she writes the specs for adding surge protectors to all substation switches. By 7:00 A.M. a situation that might have gone undetected for days or weeks, escalating into a costly crisis, is under control.[1] At first glance this might appear to be a story of how technology saved the day. But while it did play a starring role, the real hero is service, the second component of the Value Experience.

From an experience perspective, service is first and foremost about caring for a company's most valuable asset—its customer. Service can come in many forms, direct and indirect; take place in stores, homes, offices, or plants; and occur during any stage of the Experience Engagement Process. It may be a onetime event or a lifetime relationship. However, wherever, and whenever service takes place, its sole purpose is to make the customer happy. When Square D, a division of Schneider Electric, had a sales engineer on the job before the customer arrived at work, it sent a message that nothing was more important than the customer's well-being. If the plant manager had been left to deal with the situation alone, it would have been a very different story. Every business day we are faced with similar decisions. Do we go the extra mile or not? Do we spend the extra dollar or keep it for ourselves? How we answer dictates the quality of the experience we deliver to our customers and, in turn, what they give back to us. When service is good, customers are satisfied. Of course, the opposite is also true.

In mid-2001, a University of Michigan report indicated that customer satisfaction levels (of the buying public) declined for the second straight quarter, part of a downward trend that has been taking place since 1996.[2] In our opinion, these declines are based largely on poor service. It doesn't have to be this way. There are many ways to deliver good service, depending on the level of involvement a company has with its customers. Direct involvement such as the kind Square D demonstrated presents different opportunities than those available to a milk producer or a consultant, for example. It's not the type of service you provide, but the quality that matters—or, put another way, how your service impacts your customers' Value Experience.

Does your help desk really solve problems, or does it leave customers feeling frustrated and on their own? Do your front-line people communicate the importance you place on your customers, or do they just conduct business as usual? Could you make dealing with your company more pleasant, or have internal processes made your life easier and theirs more difficult? Only you can answer these questions. But whatever the state of your current service culture, it can be made better if you focus on this singular goal—*to care for the customer*. When you do, both your customers and company benefit.

Through service you can differentiate your offering, attract new customers, and enhance the value of your products. When service is done well, it also leads to customer loyalty. According to Frederick F. Reichheld, author of *The Loyalty Effect,* an increase in customer loyalty of just 5 percent can increase profitability *35 to 95 percent.*[3] Anyone would be pleased with these numbers—even at the lower end of the scale. With so much potential gain at stake, it makes sense for every business to put its service component under a microscope to determine its effectiveness. This is true even if service is not a major part of your business—everyone has at least some aspect of service in their offering, so every business can benefit by improving it. In this chapter we'll explore several service scenarios to help you determine which apply to you. Because of its somewhat elusive nature and the fact that service is both a critical and complex component, we've organized the material into four categories. These categories, based on the type of service the customer needs, are *Help Me, Serve Me, Fix Me,* and *Give Me More.* Let's start with the one that nearly every business has to deal with at one time or another: Help Me.

Help Me

HOW MANY TIMES have you heard someone in a store, on the phone, or even in the street say, "Can you help me?" How many times have you said it yourself? The fact is, not a day goes by without someone, somewhere needing help in a consumer-related matter. People have questions about products, process, or policies. They need advice or information. It may not even be your product they ask about, but still you get the question. Whether customers are asking for directions or calling a hot line on Thanksgiving Day panicked over a still-frozen turkey, they are crying out for help, and it is the role of businesses to provide it. This is Help Me service; it is the most challenging of the four categories, because by its very nature it's unpredictable. That being the case, how can you possibly deliver good service? Sometimes it's tough, but it's not impossible. Not if you understand your customers and look at service from their point of view.

When a customer needs assistance to make a purchase, use a product, or even complain, they want a quick, decisive, and appropriate response. They also want to know you care what happens to them. The most successful companies instill in their employees a reverence for the customer and offer rewards or incentives for putting the customer first.[4] Moreover, customer-centric organizations also make sure their people have the training, knowledge, and empowerment to act in the best interest of those they serve. Let's look at a major U.S. airline that combined training and knowledge to improve not only customer satisfaction but its own bottom line as well.

A Tale of Two Value Groups

A typical airline call center receives two types of calls on a regular basis: people without reservations looking for flight information and customers with reservations who want to confirm flight times, arrange special food, book seat assignments, and so on. Typically the calls are dumped to the same group of agents, requiring them to know a great deal about the entire company's operation. This of course is possible, at least in theory, but is it the best solution for the customer? The airline in our case study decided it wasn't.

During an evaluation of its call center, the airline discovered there was roughly a fifty-fifty split between the two types of calls—inquiries and assistance. It also learned that agents were overwhelmed by increasingly complex flight schedules, fares, and restrictions, making it difficult to serve either group well. This situation caused customer dissatisfaction to run rampant, and sales suffered. In fact, of the people requesting flight information, only 10 percent actually purchased a ticket. A large majority of the remainder booked with a travel agent, costing the company business.

Based on these findings the company reengineered its call center into two groups based on the two most common types of calls. Customers and prospects were now prompted to select whether they wanted flight information or required other assistance. Each internal group was given specific knowledge relating to the type of customer it would be dealing with and focused training to assist them in meeting the customer's needs. Additionally, a computerized system provided the sales group with customer profiles, allowing it to tailor the flight arrangements to each individual. Whether the frequent flier preferred a nonstop flight, an early or late flight, window or aisle seat, or a special meal, the agent was prepared with information to make the best of the flying experience. It is interesting to note that the company aligned the services to meet the needs of customers at two very different stages of the engagement process. The first group was in the evaluation stage and therefore needed much different assistance than the second group, which was in the acquisition stage. Often you can improve your service simply by recognizing which stage a group is in and adjusting accordingly.

The initial results of the airline program included a 100 percent increase in revenue-generating calls and a 50 percent increase in the average revenue per call. Because customers were handled more efficiently and effectively, the company also realized a 35 percent reduction in the average cost per call.[5] Providing employees with the training and knowledge they needed to care for their customers was key to this success. But as important as training and knowledge are in the world of service, they still may not be enough, especially when it comes to Help Me service. As we know all too well, customers always manage to come up with new ways to test our service resolve. Therefore, the best organizations not only train their employees thoroughly, they also empower them to make critical on-the-spot decisions.

Empowerment is a word that has been bandied about often in recent years, but the reality is, front-line service people typically do not have the power to give customers what they need. It is baffling to us, for instance, that a company would ask an employee to collect an overdue invoice and yet not give that person the power to correct a billing error. From customer service to shipping and sales, we consistently find that employees do not have the authority or training to deal with common requests. Instead, they often shuffle customers off to another employee, another department, and sometimes even another company.

This compartmentalization of duties not only frustrates the customer, it demoralizes employees as well. No one wants to spend her days doing half a job or listening to frustrated customers vent, but that's what happens when employees aren't permitted to take proper care of customers themselves. After eighteen years as a loyal Federal Express user, Diana closed her account. This defection happened specifically because employees were not empowered to save the relationship. Unfortunately, stories like this are all too common today.

Loyalty Lost

Shortly after moving to a new location, Diana called to request a change in her FedEx shipping and billing address. A pleasant customer service representative took down the information and assured Diana the changes were taken care of. Over the next several weeks it was business as usual. Diana called for pickups and FedEx appeared—until one afternoon in late January. It was 4:45 P.M. and she had only fifteen minutes to order a pickup for that day. The package she was sending was urgent, so when the system put her on hold, she was concerned. After several seconds, a person came on the line and informed Diana that she would not be able to schedule a pickup because her account was delinquent. Instead, she would have to go to a FedEx office and pay by cash or credit card.

Diana was shocked. According to her records the account was paid in full. After some investigation it was learned that her last payment, made several weeks earlier, had not been posted and several bills sent to the old address were never received. Understanding that mistakes sometimes happen, Diana asked if FedEx could pick up her urgent package today and then give both her and the billing office ten days to straighten out the record-keeping problems. The response was unequivocally no. She could pay the bill and FedEx would reinstate the account or she could wait until her bank statement arrived and then prove that FedEx had cashed the check. Until then, however, her credit privileges were on hold. So, after eighteen years as a good and loyal customer, Diana was left holding a critical package with instructions to prove she was once again trustworthy.

When the bank statement arrived two weeks later showing that FedEx had indeed cashed the check, she called again and was told to send a copy of the cancelled check. Unfortunately her cancelled checks are not returned with the statement. Frustrated, she refused, offering instead to give her bank information to FedEx so it could track down the misplaced payment. Once again the answer was no—to do so was against policy. In a last attempt to salvage the relationship, she asked a supervisor to call. No one ever did. Instead FedEx sent her account to collections.

Clearly FedEx did not intend for process and policy to so impede problem resolution that a long-standing customer—or any customer for that matter—would be treated in this way. What happened was a breakdown in the system, compounded by employees who were not encouraged or empowered to help. If any one of the four people Diana talked to during this meltdown period had tried to help, the outcome would have been different. Studies show that when employees have the authority to act on their own, they are more likely to provide the responses necessary to satisfy and retain customers.[6] Every company should closely examine the "Help Me" needs of its customers and provide the training and processes necessary to take care of them. The likely long-term costs of ignoring these steps are higher customer turnover and lower employee morale—both of which can directly impact the bottom line.

Serve Me

E VERY TIME a customer goes to a McDonald's, stands in line at a ticket counter, or places a routine order, she is saying, "Serve Me." This type of encounter is typically associated with classic service purveyors such as restaurants, dry cleaners, lawyers, and doctors, but it also includes common experiences like paying for the purchase. Unlike Help Me service, which is often unpredictable, Serve Me tends to be just the opposite. Routine and predictable, it is much easier to control than the Help Me category. For instance, a restaurant will always seat customers, take their orders, and deliver food to the table. These events occur every time with every customer. This is also true in the case of professional services, such as medical care. When a patient goes to a doctor's office he or she may have unique symptoms, but the general process is still the same—sign in, sit in the waiting room, have your weight and temperature taken, talk to the nurse, repeat the same information for the doctor, schedule diagnostic tests, and so forth. Whether you run a hospital or a hamburger joint, Serve Me is built upon routine. In chapter 4 we discussed process attributes, which of course are central here, but as we examine the Serve Me category, we want to look at an added dimension of this type of service—customer expectations.

Great Expectations

Expectations are an important part of the Value Experience in general, but this is even more true of service. When a customer goes to a store, calls a sales rep or service technician, or shows up for an appointment, he expects a certain level of service. When his expectations are met he is pleased; when they aren't he's dissatisfied. Those expectations are based largely on what people are looking for from the company and its offering. For example, with common, frequently used services, customers look for efficiency and affordability, but they also value consistency. For more occasional or special services people still expect efficiency, but they also want to be treated with a little extra care.

Let's say that every morning on the way to work you stop for coffee; every Thursday you go to McDonald's for lunch; and every Saturday is dry cleaning day. For these ordinary routines you have well-established expectations of how the encounters will go and there is comfort, order, and meaning in this consistency. In fact, for many people such experiences serve as anchors in what might otherwise be a day full of chaos.

So what happens when these routine expectations are not met? Often customers feel out of sorts and, reasonable or not, usually look for someone or something to hang their discomfort on. Have you ever made the statement, "I knew it was going to be a bad day when . . ."? That "when" could be "when it took half an hour to get my coffee" or "when I got to the office and there was snow piled in my parking space." If customers can ascribe a "when" to your service, you lose. This is why a company like McDonald's concentrates so much of its effort on consistently delivering its product, day after day, store after store. It understands people value the fact that they can count on a Serve Me experience that consistently meets their expectations. If your business delivers this type of service, it's imperative to determine what role you play in your customers' daily routines and do what you can to make life easier. With service, it's the little things that often count the most, even if the service is occasional.

For many people, going to an expensive restaurant happens only once or twice a year. The same is true of vacations, visits to the hospital, or conferences. These events are less common and thus carry expectations that service will be special. It doesn't matter if there are dozens if not hundreds of other people having the same experience, for each customer it is an out-of-the-ordinary happening. Cruise lines have done an exceptional job of creating a special service experience and we can all learn a great deal from their example.

Cruise lines know that when people book a cruise, they are hoping for the vacation of a lifetime. Their customers set aside time months in advance, prepay for the trip, and even buy whole new wardrobes just for the occasion. Clearly, expectations are high. But since a cruise lasts several days, cruise lines know they can't possibly sustain a "once-in-a-lifetime" experience every hour of the day and night. To help them do precisely what is needed precisely when it's needed, many lines turn to science. According to behavioral scientists, when customers remember an experience they don't recall every single event. Instead they remember only a few events vividly, especially the ending, and gloss over the rest. In other words, they remember snapshots, not movies.[7] Therefore, the longer the event, the more important it is to manage the sequences and snapshots.

Studies have also found that people favor a sequence of events that improve over time. People prefer to first lose $5 at the blackjack table and then win $10 rather than win $10 and lose $5.[8] Using this information, cruise ships have carefully constructed a sequence of events to provide increasingly more pleasant snapshots, starting out each day slowly and then building to the finale. This end-of-day experience might include raffles, contests, or a dinner show; whatever the choice, the customer falls asleep feeling that she's having a great time. The end of the cruise also finishes on a high note with an elaborate "captain's dinner" and a departure gift when home port is reached. These same techniques can be applied to any Serve Me process. Even hospitals are beginning to recognize that by viewing service as a process and then taking steps to manage snapshots and sequences, customer expectations are not only met but surpassed.

Seeing the Whole Picture

Over the past decade, for example, medical industry studies have found that there is a distinct disparity between how a patient evaluates an individual procedure versus the process as a whole.[9] The doctor may have been attentive and responsive, the X-ray technician friendly and informative, the nurse gentle and caring, but after sitting in the hallway between events for two hours, the overall experience gets a pretty low rating. When no single individual is responsible for patient care from beginning to end, you can see how this happens: Each nurse, doctor, and department is focused solely on a single area of expertise and has little regard for the total service process.

One hospital that has taken steps to remedy this situation is Reading Rehabilitation. In the mid-1990s it implemented patient care coordinators as part of its patient-focused care initiative. The care coordinators serve as case managers for a group of patients and are responsible for monitoring and managing the entire patient care process. They are involved in every event, from check-in to checkout, to ensure that the process moves along smoothly and the patient is properly cared for. They also make sure the myriad of doctors and nurses who might interact with a single patient fully understand that patient's situation as well as the role of the other caregivers. The result of this initiative was a hospital quality rating of 8.7 versus a national benchmark of 8.0 and teamwork rating of 8.8 versus a national rank of 7.8.[10]

These signs that even our most internally focused industries such as health care are beginning to realize the importance of improving service to customers are encouraging. However, for every company that embraces a renewed service ethic, there seems to be another that decides Serve Me means "Serve Thyself." Self-serve has become a common trend in the last few years, and while we are not opposed to self-serve as a concept, it has rapidly become one of the most abused service techniques—especially when it is done primarily to reduce costs.[11] When this is the motive, the company may cut dollar costs, but the price it pays in customer equity can be greater. If you don't think so, just ask First National Bank of Chicago.

In an effort to decrease costs by reducing teller staff, in June 1995 First National Bank implemented a $3 fee for any teller-assisted transaction. The idea was to motivate customers to use electronic methods of banking, which were less labor intensive. Although the idea looked good on paper, the error in the bank's thinking was soon apparent. Customers were appalled. Within days the bank made local, national, and international headlines. Other banks ran radio ads berating its approach and explaining that *they* would not charge you a fee for talking with them. Unhappy customers inundated First National Bank with phone calls and many visited the bank to ask for an explanation. Hopefully they weren't charged $3 to voice their complaints. Although the bank got a lot of free publicity, it probably would have gladly passed on the exposure.[12]

This extreme example of forcing self-serve on customers is not the norm, of course, but we use it to illustrate this point: When you ask the customer to accept a sacrifice without a reward, everyone loses. By its very nature, self-serve is a sacrifice; you are asking customers to care for themselves instead of you caring for them. Therefore, if you want to maintain the value of your offering you have two choices. Either make sure self-serve offers them a reward such as convenience and efficiency (as Kroger did with its self-serve checkout lanes) or decrease another sacrifice, such as price. When considering this approach, even for cost-cutting reasons, check it out on the experience event matrix first to make sure you're not decreasing the value of your product.

We'll offer one last thought on self-serve—it should always be considered as an integral part of the Value Experience, not just a point solution. Before heading down this path, ask yourself if you really want to miss the opportunity to touch a customer personally. If you're competing on price the answer may be yes; otherwise you might want to consider caring for your customers as no one else can—even themselves.

Fix Me

TYPICALLY we think of the next type of service as repair or "fix-it." We have dubbed it "Fix Me" because whenever something is broken, be it a product or a service delivery, the customer—or at least your relationship with the customer—is damaged as well. For example, when a VCR suddenly quits working in the middle of a movie, eating a favorite tape, it's not just the VCR that has been affected. The customer also suffers. If during a Help Me or Serve Me episode the customer is neglected or abused by poor service, this also requires repair. No matter how the customer ended up in this category, through act of God or act of company, it's your job to ease the pain—sometimes literally.

Managing Customer Pain

Pain management has received much attention within the medical industry, and numerous studies have been conducted to evaluate how best to deal with it. Of most interest to us was one study that surprisingly showed that patients giving blood rated the pain lower when they were allowed to select the arm blood was drawn from.[13] Although giving the patient choice in this case was mostly symbolic, it allowed the patient to exercise some control in an often stressful event. When you think about it, this same concept applies to any situation in which the patient or customer is in pain. When something bad happens, no matter how minor, none of us likes to feel totally at the mercy of someone else.

How many times have you called a service organization to schedule a repair and been told which day you have to take off work to accommodate the organization's schedule? And how often has your company felt the need to spend great amounts of money on contracts for highly available service, just to make sure you have some control over when repairs are made? Probably more often than you care to think about. To remedy this problem, some companies have taken the concept of enlisting the customer's participation in "pain management" and applied it to the service call arena, with great success.

Xerox was receiving numerous complaints from its customers that repairs weren't happening fast enough and decided action was needed to resolve the situation. The obvious answer was to increase service staff, but instead it looked a little closer and decided to give customers more of a say in the service delivery process. Its current service contracts provided a specific response time, ranging from one hour to next day, based on the level of service the customer had selected. Faster response, higher contract cost. It didn't matter whether the machine was completely down or there was only a minor problem; if the service contract required next-day response, that's what the customer got.

Since this clearly wasn't working, Xerox eliminated the multitude of contracts with different response commitments and converted to a single contract with customer-defined response time. Under the new approach, each time the customer called in she was allowed to identify her need on a scale from routine to critical. Service personnel would then arrive faster for a critical call than a less urgent one. By involving the customer in the service delivery process Xerox not only increased customer satisfaction but surprisingly found fewer service personnel were needed. Rather than take advantage of the situation and define every call as critical, the customer was more interested in having a choice than instantaneous response.[14] Turning control over to the customer as Xerox did is one aspect of pain management; another is reducing, and even preventing, the pain.

Preventing Customer Pain

Let's return to the medical industry for a moment. A study showed that the majority of patients having their blood pressure checked by a doctor experienced either higher or lower blood pressure than their "normal" ambulatory readings.[15] Further analysis showed there was a reason for this pattern. When having their blood pressure checked in a doctor's office or hospital, patients typically responded in one of two ways. They were either at ease and relaxed (what safer place to be than with a doctor?) or anxious about the results of the doctor's examination. The blood pressure of the first group typically dropped, while the second group saw a higher reading. Which group would you rather have your customers in? Obviously the first. So what can you do to make sure your customers are confident and relaxed, knowing you will take care of their problems? The key to achieving this ideal state is service guarantees.

Simply put, a service guarantee says you will perform as promised and if for some reason you can't or don't, the customer will be taken care of and maybe even compensated for her pain. The objective here is to give customers peace of mind before they ever need Fix Me service, so that if they do, they approach the event more relaxed than anxious. The following service guarantee, one of the best we have seen, is included in the "owner's manual" that comes with each Tilley Endurables Hat.

> *If you ever find the Hat to be less than the best for any reason, we will repair or replace your Hat for free. If your Tilley Hat ever wears out, we'll replace it free! Bring it to any store that sells the Hat and you'll be given a new one. If you'd like to keep your worn-out Hat, I'm sure that can be arranged.*

There are several reasons why Tilley's service guarantee has such a strong impact. First, it is unconditional and easy to read. If you have to inject a lot of conditions, don't waste your time; the guarantee will not have the desired effect. To a customer, conditions mean loopholes that allow you to get out of the agreement. The second reason the Tilley guarantee works so well is that it is personal. People want to deal with people, not faceless organizations. A contract between the customer and your local store has much more impact than an impersonal corporate decree that looks like a lawyer wrote it. We're not saying guarantees can't be centrally developed, but as in the case of Tilley's suggestion to "bring it to any store," the customer should feel it is backed by a personal, and in this case local, commitment. Another way you can use service guarantees is to create a partnership between company and customers to make sure you rarely have to use it. Why would you do this? Because sometimes it's not the product or company that creates the problem, it's the customer.

"Bugs" Burger Bug Killers (BBBK), a national pest-extermination company with thousands of hotel and restaurant clients, asked itself what obstacles stood in the way of fully guaranteeing pest elimination.

Unfortunately, the answer to the question was the customer. It was often the customer's poor cleaning and storage practices that led to repeat infestation. Tough situation, but by involving the customer in the pest prevention process and requiring a hotel or restaurant to meet certain sanitary standards to qualify, it was able to guarantee the outcome of its service in a very complete way:

> (1) *You don't owe one penny until all pests on your premises have been eradicated. (2) If you are ever dissatisfied with BBBK's service, you will receive a refund for up to 12 months of the company's services—plus fees for another exterminator of your choice for the next year. (3) If a guest spots a pest on your premises, BBBK will pay for the guest's meal or room, send a letter of apology, and pay for a future meal or stay. (4) If your facility is closed down due to the presence of roaches or rodents, BBBK will pay any fines, as well as all lost profits, plus $5,000."* [16]

This guarantee keeps the customers' blood pressure nicely in the normal range, even though they typically pay up to ten times more for the company's services. As for BBBK, it has a disproportionately high market share within its operating area and, happily, it rarely has to pay out on its guarantee.[17]

If you don't currently offer a good service guarantee, you should. Start the same way BBBK did and ask yourself what obstacles stand in the way of guaranteeing your service. As with BBBK, the hurdle might be the customer, but more often than not it's internal. Unfortunately, most companies are often their own worst enemies. To avoid this kind of self-destruction, seek out and then prevent as many problem areas as possible. That way when the inevitable problem occurs—service guarantee or not, you have a suitable remedy in place to meet it head-on.

Just as you wouldn't put a cast on a scratched arm or a Band-Aid on a fractured one, service remedies should be appropriate, relative, and flexible. Research on what customers perceive as an appropriate remedy indicates the answer depends on whether the service process failed or just wasn't handled properly.[18] In a situation where a Help Me customer was turned into a Fix Me customer because of a rude sales clerk, the customer expects a sincere apology. On the other hand, we recently witnessed an incident where the security sensor wasn't removed from a garment and the customer had to make a second trip to the store to resolve the problem. In this case the woman appropriately expected material compensation for the process error. Each type of error requires the right remedy and nothing more. The first customer shouldn't be given a discount, unless of course the employee was downright insulting, while the second shouldn't have to settle for an "I'm sorry" when she was so clearly inconvenienced.

The remedy should be relative to the magnitude of the error. Domino's Pizza found this out when it promised delivery within thirty minutes or the pizza was free. Customers were hesitant to take advantage of this offer because they felt it was too generous, but when Domino's reduced it to a $3 off coupon, people felt more comfortable and thus took the offer more seriously.[19] If you offer more than is required, the customer is uncomfortable; if you offer too little, he is dissatisfied, so it's important to get it right. This is where your well-trained employees from the Help Me group can be of great service. Since not all situations can be identified in advance, it is important to allow front-line employees, or at least first-level managers, to use their discretion in supplying remedies. If you allow them to be flexible you are more likely to have a satisfied customer—one with whom you will have the opportunity to try our final type of service.

Give Me More

WHILE EACH of the first three types of service can add value when done well, the last type of service—what we call Give Me More—is strictly value-added and employed most often to provide a competitive advantage. There are two general approaches for adding value with this type of service and both are process related. The first approach addresses a broad group of customers, all dealing with a common process. The second approach customizes the company process for each customer, providing individualized service. Both require refinement of process attributes to succeed. Let's take a closer look at two companies that have each added value through Give Me More service.

Our first company, National Semiconductor, did this by improving a common customer process.[20]

Engineering Experience Improvement

One of the interesting aspects of the semiconductor business is that design engineers, although not directly involved in the purchasing process, have a sizable influence on purchasing decisions. The parts they select early during the evaluate stage often determine the final component selection as the product goes into production. Therefore, they form a key audience for semiconductor manufacturers and one National Semiconductor decided was ripe with opportunity for customer process improvement. By helping design engineers make better choices, it would move upstream in the purchasing process.

In the late 1990s Phil Gibson, vice president of Web business for National Semiconductor, led a team focused on the customer design process for power supplies. It found that most design engineers used a four-step process: choose a part, create a design, analyze a design, and build a prototype. From initial design to final configuration this process could take months, and evaluation of alternatives was typically limited by time constraints. The result of the team's efforts was Webench, the industry's first comprehensive Web environment for power supply designers, including the Power Supply Design Assistant, which walks the engineer through a four-step process. Let's log on and see how it works.

First we are asked to select our design requirements—for example, power in and power out. After making our selections we are presented with a list of chips, including detailed specifications and price. Next we select the specific IC we want to use, and upon clicking the design button receive a parts list. This list includes components from other manufacturers, operating values, and a schematic. Since a couple of the operating values don't meet our design needs, we can easily try again with a few simple clicks. After finalizing our design a sophisticated application licensed by National allows us to run real-time simulations, including interactive probes and the ability to add personal notes to the results. The final solution is saved in a private portfolio that offers the ability to e-mail links to colleagues.

We were impressed, but how about real design engineers? According to David Katz, senior design engineer at Motorola, Webench was a winner: "I think the tool has great potential for accelerating device selection, as well as facilitating rapid prototyping of circuit blocks. Given its broad variety of analysis options and intuitive user interface, it can easily save weeks worth of part searches and design simulations."[21] He's obviously not the only one feeling this way. In its first year of operation, more than twenty thousand power supplies were designed on the site and by December 1998, 2,600 sample parts were being ordered per day. Although the initial order might consist of only a handful of components, Gibson points out that "one integrated-socket win with Nokia translates into forty million units for us."[22]

With design time per power supply reduced by an average of fifty hours (according to National), customer savings were estimated at $135 million in the first year and a half Webench was online. The result is a Give Me More service that leaves design engineers unlikely to go elsewhere for their power supply components. Our next company took the second approach by modifying its process attributes to provide individualized service.

Keeping Each Customer in Clear Focus

The Paris Miki retail chain has six hundred stores in Japan and another sixty throughout Asia, Europe, the United States, and Australia. With sales of nearly $750 billion, it is the world's second largest optical chain.[23] But it's not just large; it is also unique. Buying glasses has long been a trying process, literally: evaluate your choices, try a pair on, and repeat step two until you are satisfied. The process at Paris Miki is much different, thanks to an interactive software program that assists the customer in selecting eyewear. Upon entering one of its stores, the customer is greeted by an associate who takes a digital picture of the customer; the computer then measures the distance between her eyes and the length of her nose. The customer then chooses from a list of sixty image words such as "glamorous," "intelligent," "sporty," "sexy," "distinctive," and "professional" to describe the look she desires. Based on the customer's facial shape and the selected adjectives, the artificial intelligence system recommends frames and lenses. The results are displayed onscreen over the digital image of the customer's face, allowing her to "try on" several pairs without leaving her seat. The customer can even customize the eyewear if the look is close but not exactly right. The whole process takes between fifteen and twenty minutes and custom glasses are delivered within two weeks. According to Carol Norbeck, Paris Miki vice president, its personalized approach is very well accepted. In fact, more than 50 percent of customers at the company's Seattle store came on a friend's recommendation.

Rite Aid Has Right Aid

Although unique ideas like the two just cited are a great start, for service excellence to move from concept to reality also requires a unique company. Whether the service is Help Me, Serve Me, Fix Me, or Give Me More, success requires commitment and a strong customer-centric culture. In an article that appeared in the *Marketing News* of the American Marketing Association, Rite Aid, one of the nation's leading drugstore chains with annual revenues of $14 billion, was featured for an incident of exceptional customer service.[24] The real story, however, isn't just this onetime event, it's the culture the company has in place to make the event possible.

One summer, a day after his fifty-first birthday, Marty Pay, a Farmers Insurance agent in Tehachapi, California, developed what he thought was a bad case of heartburn during a bike ride. Before taking an antacid, he called his pharmacy to ask if it would interact with his diabetes medication. The Rite Aid pharmacist, Ronde Snell, asked about the nature of the pain, whether he'd had heartburn before, and a little about his medical history.

Based on this ten-minute conversation, Snell told Pay that she thought he could be experiencing not heartburn but heart pain, a precursor to a heart attack. She suggested that he go to the emergency room to have it checked out. A couple of hours later Snell called the local hospital to see what had happened and learned that her customer had not come in. Concerned, she tracked him down at his office and told him to go immediately to the emergency room. Once there, doctors learned that Pay had a 95 percent blockage of one artery. Within days he underwent an angioplasty.

This customer service story was made possible by a culture that nurtured and empowered caring in employees. It began two years earlier when marketing research showed that customers wanted a more personal pharmacist-customer relationship, and Rite Aid listened. "Even though it's a chain of 3,600 stores, customers view each store as *their* pharmacy," says John Learish, Rite Aid's vice president of marketing. Knowing this is what customers thought, Rite Aid was determined to make it a reality. To that end, company executives visited pharmacies and interviewed and observed their pharmacists at work nationwide. The executives then took the important step of streamlining processes and procedures to free up more time for pharmacists. For example, the company implemented a "basket" system that takes a prescription form and all related documents and components and places them in a basket until the filled prescription reaches the customer. It's simple but effective in saving time, rounding up all the components necessary to do the job. New processes also freed pharmacists of certain administrative duties so they could spend more time with the customers, such as Pay.

Other Rite Aid policies such as e-mail alerts about drug recalls or other changes also help druggists take better care of customers. Snell recalls that when Bayer's Baycol (a cholesterol drug) was taken off the market, many customers called with questions. "We had information for them the same day," she says. For employees this quick response meant fewer callbacks, and for customers it meant less anxiety.

Superior customer service benefited Rite Aid's image as well as its patrons. In 2001 the company launched a six-month national TV ad campaign showcasing pharmacist customer service stories like Snell's. In addition to reinforcing Rite Aid's customer focus, Learish says, "It also sets the expectation of what our deliverable is among pharmacists, and challenges Rite Aid employees to live up to those expectations."

This type of customer-focused culture fostered by Rite Aid is no less than what every customer deserves. Whether you want your service to help, fix, nurture, or add value, it all starts with cultural commitment.

As difficult as this might seem at first, there are many tools available to make this commitment easier. Use what you know about your customers both as individuals and as Value Groups. Identify the Experience Engagement Process stage they are in. This information will help you direct your resources more effectively and solicit the best internal assistance. If customers are in the discover or evaluate stage, marketing may provide valuable insight. For integrate stage service programs, your front-line employees should be involved.

Have some fun and engage as many people as possible in exercises to focus the company on service. You could draft a service guarantee for your company. Be extreme. For example, state that as a company every customer call will be answered on the first ring or that 100 percent of shipments will be correct. Then identify any obstacles stopping you from making this guarantee. You may be surprised how many are easily eliminated. You could also develop a list of questions a customer might ask as part of Help Me service. Be creative. Then take the realistic ones and see if employees know or can easily find the answers they need to deliver the desired service. For each type of service there are comparable exercises your company can do to increase the awareness and effectiveness of this critical component of the Value Experience. If you nurture a customer service environment, before long every employee will be an ambassador of service. When that happens customer loyalty isn't far behind.

PRICELESS ROADMAP—CHAPTER 5

- ➤ Identify the type of service that is appropriate to your business and where you think you can have the greatest impact on the Value Experience.

- ➤ Create a list of the common customer situations that occur during this type of service.

- ➤ Identify the experience events involving interaction between company and customer and in which stage of the EEP they occur.

CHAPTER SIX

Surroundings

THE ENVIRONMENT COMPONENT

I N 1968 THE MUSIC WORLD WAS STUNNED WHEN THE newest Beatles album appeared on the scene in nothing more than a milky white jacket. At a time when psychedelic flower-power imagery ruled, its stripped-down minimalist look was mysterious and provocative. The double album sold an unprecedented two million copies in its first week of release, reaching four million albums sold by month's end. This phenomenon was fueled by the unusual jacket, which was not only distinctive for its day, but was also numbered sequentially as though it were a limited-edition collector's print. Street rumor had it that only the original release would have the coveted numbered cover; whether it was true or not (it was), die-hard fans didn't want to be left out. In short order the album, which was officially titled *The Beatles,* became known as the "White Album" and even today is referred to by that name. Of all the Beatles albums released by Apple Records, this one still commands the highest collector's price today. This bit of packaging genius was a case of a product's surroundings bringing unexpected and lasting value. But that's not always the case, as we'll see on our exploration of the third and final component of the Value Experience—environment.[1]

When we speak about environment as it relates to consumption, we're referring to any external element that supports the delivery, sale, and in some cases, use of a product. These elements include packaging—such as an album cover, labeling, and displays—as well as retail spaces and the places where services are provided. In most cases environmental elements do not directly affect how a product functions, but they can exert a powerful influence on individual experience events and therefore on the Value Experience.

For example, we know an aspirin bottle has nothing to do with how well the medicine inside relieves a headache. But if you're a senior and the child-resistant cap is too difficult to open, it causes frustration and annoyance, and delays pain relief. The result is a sacrifice—not a good situation for the ailing customer or the company that relies on repeat business. On the other hand, if the bottle cap employs one of the easier-to-open technologies such as squeeze tabs, the product has a chance to work its magic sooner and avoids the stigma of a sacrifice. In this case we have a satisfied customer and a company that has eliminated an avenue of competitive assault through environment.

Many such opportunities exist to delight the customer and protect or enhance business through this often-underestimated component. We'll look at some of them in this chapter and suggest guidelines to help you evaluate your own offering's effectiveness in two distinct areas. The first is the microenvironment, or those elements that immediately surround a product such as containers and labels. Microenvironments most often impact acquire and integration experiences. The second is the macroenvironment, or the places in which products are sold and delivered. Primarily focused on acquisition, macroenvironments can also be part of the integration stage, especially for service products.

As we look at both, we'll see how different companies have used environment to gain a competitive edge, safeguard business, build customer loyalty, and even open up new markets. As with product and service, the role environment plays in your company will be unique, but as you read think about the environment-related aspects of your offering and how they add to or detract from your customer's Value Experience.

It's a Small World after All

S OMETIMES it's the little things that count the most. This certainly
is the case with microenvironment. Packaging, labels, inserts,
point-of-purchase displays, and even those annoying antitheft devices
attached to clothing in stores are all part of the microenvironment of a
product. If it touches or is included with the product but isn't a part of
the product itself, then we count it as a piece of this small world. With
so many possible elements in this category, we selected two, packaging
and labels, to illustrate how macroenvironment relates to the greater experience.[2] This focus doesn't mean other elements such as displays or
hang tags, shopping bags, and warranty cards are not important. They
are. But if you apply the same principle of using them to help, not hin-
der, an experience you'll be able to evaluate their effectiveness as it applies to your own products.

Dressing Products for Success

In a perfect world every product container would be easy to open, protect goods from damage, provide just the right information, seduce the
customer into buying, and differentiate the item from the competition.[3]
When everything is really going right, packaging is also hassle-free for
retailers and adds minimal cost to the final price. But since the world is
rarely perfect, it's no wonder packaging can be one of the most difficult
challenges a company faces.

As consumers, we deal with product packaging every day. Whether
they are on a store shelf, at home in our cupboards, or in the office supply cabinet, we are surrounded by containers. Unfortunately, for every
good packaging design created, there seem to be as many poor ones. It's
safe to say there isn't a consumer alive who hasn't been terrorized by containers that are hard to handle, difficult or confusing to open, and in-
convenient to store or dispose of. Why is this? What customer, for
instance, actually likes the heavy molded plastic that encases everything

from garden shears to hair dryers? This packaging is so difficult to open, it's clear the companies that use it have never observed their customers struggling with it. The same is true of the cellophane that encases DVDs, CDs, and similar products. Without an easy-open strip, it takes a knife to open both.

We know businesses don't go out of their way to abuse customers, and we must assume they want people to use their products. On the other hand, in many cases they aren't consciously trying to please the customer, either. When companies use packaging in a deliberate manner to increase value, however, the rewards to both customer and company can be astonishing. Many people are familiar with the story of how Pepsi took the crown from Coca-Cola in the mid-1980s. It's a classic microenvironment success story.[4]

In the late 1960s a Pepsi-Cola marketing team decided to take a serious look at how consumers behaved when they bought and drank Pepsi-Cola. The in-home study involved 350 families who were given the opportunity to buy Pepsi and any competitive product at discount prices over a period of several weeks. When the results were in, the researchers discovered that no matter how many bottles of Pepsi were purchased, consumers drank all they had. This was an excellent testimonial for product quality. What was even more interesting, however, was the fact that the total amount of soda purchased was not determined by brand preferences; it was decided by the test subject's ability to comfortably carry the product home.

Armed with this interesting bit of insight and determined to challenge its archrival, Coca-Cola, in retail outlets, the company focused on its packaging. Before long, lightweight plastic replaced glass, larger two-liter recyclable bottles replaced small ones, and multipacks of twelve bottles replaced the traditional six-packs. These easy-carry options were exactly what the customer wanted and they worked like a charm. Given a choice, people preferred the new packaging. So in addition to increasing its own sales, Pepsi was able to convert a major Coke strength—its small, distinctive (but heavy) hourglass bottle—into a sacrifice people were not willing to accept once given an alternative.

Making its product easier to acquire was enough to get Pepsi's foot in the consumer door and give it an opportunity to prove its product. As we know from taste tests, once people tried Pepsi, they preferred it to the taste of Coke. By 1976, Pepsi was the single largest soft drink brand sold in American supermarkets. In 1978 Pepsi took its innovation one step further, introducing twelve-pack aluminum cans. By 1980 it was number one in sales for the entire take-home market, which included supermarkets along with all other carry-home outlets. Because of this environment-focused coup, Pepsi would hold onto this crown for over half a decade.

Packaging breakthroughs such as this, which focus on a particular aspect of the customer experience, can be a powerful differentiator, as Pepsi discovered. The story also reminds us that as innovations in materials and design become available or customer lifestyles change, companies should revisit their packaging to ensure that it's keeping pace with the times. Since the first appearance of the curved Coke bottle in 1915 (introduced to distinguish the soft drink from its competitors, no less), grocery shopping had changed considerably. Coke's primary grocery store Value Group no longer consisted of housewives shopping at neighborhood stores, but harried working women trudging through supermarkets and several acres of parking lot. For this shopper, Coca-Cola's heavy, old-style bottles left the door wide open for competitive assault. Even with something as seemingly unimportant as a container, we can't rest on our laurels. This caution applies as much to the commercial world as it does to the consumer market.

In the latter part of the twentieth century, businesses found themselves faced with governmental, environmental, and cost-containment issues that directly impacted packaging strategy. This was especially true in manufacturing and assembly operations, where thousands of parts might be needed to create one product. In order to address these issues, several packaging companies, working with their customers, began exploring the use of returnable containers. A returnable container is one the assembler can unload and then send back empty to the original supplier. Most returnable containers are made of plastic, which can be formed to almost any shape for any application and be used over and over again. This means a packaging solution can be easily customized to meet a specific need. For instance, one assembler might want handheld containers that operators can carry to a workstation or line-side rack. Another might want bulk containers, which hold large volumes of material weighing up to 2,500 pounds.[5]

Thus, from a value perspective, the reusable-container solution is able to take a costly, management-intensive part of the microenvironment and use it to deliver convenience, efficiency, satisfaction, and even an enhanced relationship. By allowing the company to choose the method of packing that is best for its situation, parts vendors can transform themselves from suppliers of goods to partners that contribute to their customer's success. This not only brings value to the customer, but also makes it more difficult for competitors to penetrate the account. It's a win-win. Of course, the opposite can also be true.

A medical devices service company had a run-in with a vendor because the supplier wanted to change how it delivered plastic tubing for a popular piece of medical equipment. The materials had always been delivered in precut lengths, which made it convenient for field service reps to take the tubing with them on service calls. In order to save on transportation costs, however, the manufacturer wanted to begin shipping the tubing in large rolls. This meant the customer would have to hand-cut the lengths in its shop, resulting in both a major inconvenience as well as added costs for time and labor. No amount of arguing would persuade the manufacturer to change its mind, and because the customer was only midway through a long-term contract it could not break, it had little immediate recourse.[6] Clearly the manufacturer wasn't thinking long-term. Just because the customer was locked into a contract at the time doesn't mean that will always be the case. Most bullied customers bolt at the first opportunity.

We find that nearly every business has similar shortsighted microenvironment practices and that quite often its customers give clear signals as to what they are. Even if yours haven't so far, observing how customers interact with a product often uncovers ways in which we can enhance value by making the packing more user-friendly.

Industry-leading AlpineAire Foods, a manufacturer of freeze-dried foods for backpacking and camping, knows its customers are very conscious about how much weight they have to carry. To improve the carrying experience, AlpineAire packages its product in a foil-lined pouch that can double as a pot. A camper only needs to add boiling water to the package, stir, reseal the container, wait five minutes, and then dig in. This creative use of packaging based on customer use allows outdoorsmen to carry less and still enjoy a good, hot meal (they even have Bananas Foster). Best of all, there are no dishes to wash afterward.

Several of AlpineAire's competitors also use this trek-friendly design, but one, MSR Mountain, has taken the convenience a step further by making its cook-in packaging burnable, thus eliminating the need to carry the empty bag back out or find a suitable disposal place. Because MSR doesn't have the breadth of product line available from AlpineAire, it's doubtful the leader is in immediate danger; but then again, that's probably what Coca-Cola thought as well.

When you look at your own packaging, ask yourself if there is some improvement like the one MSR developed that can add value to your product or, at the very least, eliminate a sacrifice. The first place to begin is where the consumer starts: opening (and then closing) the package. Nothing is more annoying than being unable to easily access a product for which you just paid good money. Other factors to consider are transporting, use, storage, and disposal. Also look for extended uses, such as the package-turned-cooking-pot and the reusable containers we discussed earlier. Turn to your customers to give you direction. But don't just ask; observe them interacting with your packaging.

In order to test the efficacy of child-resistant caps, regulations require that companies observe fifty kids between the ages of forty-two and fifty-one months in a room for ten minutes as well as one hundred adults between the ages of fifty and seventy years old in another room for five minutes, all trying to open their containers. Packaging passes if 85 percent of the children cannot gain access to the medication in the allotted time and 90 percent of the adults can open the package in five minutes and reclose it in one minute.[7] We're not suggesting that taking five minutes to open a package is acceptable; it's not, but the testing concept isn't a bad one. If more companies tested their packaging for customer friendliness, we'd all be happier consumers. Sometimes, though, it doesn't take a whole package to bring a little something extra to the value table. One of the earliest and most engaging microenvironment stories we've uncovered involves not a package, but a label and a gutsy French baron willing to fly in the face of tradition.

The Art of Labeling

Before 1924, it was customary for vineyards to sell each vintage in barrels to wine merchants who would then mature, bottle, label, and market the wine. Once the wine merchant took over, the vintner lost control and therefore any interest in the finished product. This apathy extended to the appearance of the bottle and, of course, the label. With no one to tell them otherwise, the opportunistic merchants often created labels where their names were at least as prominent as the owners, if not more so. As any brand-conscious company knows, this wasn't doing the vineyards a bit of good. In fact, if any branding was taking place, it was the merchant who more often than not received the rewards.

In 1924 Baron Philippe de Rothschild, owner of the then moderately recognized Mouton-Rothschild vineyard, took exception to the tradition. Unhappy at losing control over his product, the baron made the revolutionary decision to bottle his entire harvest before it left his property. This was a momentous step, making the owner responsible for the final product that reached the customer. But with the responsibility also came opportunity. If the chateau controlled the wine, it could also control the label. From then on that small square of paper took on a new importance and new function. Once the merchant's mark, the label now became the trademark, the proof of origin, the guarantee of quality of the vineyard.

To celebrate this departure from tradition, de Rothschild commissioned the famous poster designer, Jean Carlu, to design an exciting new label for the 1924 vintage. It instantly set Mouton-Rothschild apart from every other Bordeaux region wine. This in and of itself was a coup that boosted the reputation and visibility of de Rothschild's wine, but the real genius came twenty years later. To commemorate the victory of the Allies in World War II and to mark a new beginning for his beloved France, the baron asked the young painter Philippe Julian to produce a graphic design based on the "V" sign made famous by Winston Churchill during the war. The new label created such a stir not only among wine lovers, but art lovers as well, that from 1946 onward a contemporary artist has been commissioned to illustrate the label each year.

Over the past fifty years such renowned artists as Salvador Dali (1958), Joan Miro (1969), Marc Chagall (1970), Pablo Picasso (1973), and

Andy Warhol (1975) have designed labels for Mouton-Rothschild. In exchange for their creations, the artists receive five cases of wine from the current vintage as well as five additional cases, which they can select from the cellar. In dollar terms, this labeling innovation hasn't cost the company a great deal—genius doesn't have to be expensive—but the rewards have been tremendous. Even when Mouton-Rothschild is having an off-vintage year, it still commands the highest prices for wines from the Bordeaux region. As the *Wine Spectator* explains: "This extra value can be chalked up to the label and its art rather than the quality of the wine."[8] In essence, Mouton-Rothschild has extended the value of its offering beyond the product itself through environment. This added value allows the company to insulate itself from competitive assault, whether it is from product quality, innovation, marketing, or price-cutting. And of course, the customer gets to own an amazing work of micro-art.[9]

Labels are used for more than branding and collecting, of course. They also provide needed information such as directions for use, material or ingredient statements, nutrition facts, and cautions.[10] This information empowers customers by allowing them to make informed decisions and helps ensure that the product is used properly, increasing the chances of a satisfactory user experience. When viewed in this light, we can see the importance of presenting information in an intelligible and logical manner. This means using type that is large enough for the target audience to read—remember, the population is aging and so is their eyesight. It also means presenting the most useful information first. We compared the labeling on two different pain-relief products—Motrin IB and Aleve. The Motrin bottle was about half the size of the Aleve bottle, yet it did a better job of presenting information than the larger container. On the Motrin bottle the directions for use were presented on one side of the bottle. All the necessary warnings and indications were offered on the other side. Both are important, but let's face it, when one is in pain directions for use take precedence, and Motrin's were easy to find.

The Aleve bottle, however, presented marketing information first, under the guise of "Uses"—even though the front of the bottle clearly indicated that the product was a pain reliever and fever reducer. We had to read to the middle of label to find directions for use. What's unfortunate is the fact that the makers of Aleve went the extra mile in providing an easy-open bottle, only to fall short on the small details of its label. We see this all too often. A company will pay attention to some details and ignore other, equally important aspects. For a true Value Experience, all the fine points must be addressed, no matter how small. For example, one company began putting the customer's purchase order numbers on shipping labels, making it easier for receiving and purchasing to log in and track orders. Nordstrom includes a postage-paid return label in reusable packaging to make mail-order returns easier. Sometimes these courtesies add only a small amount to overhead, but the benefit to customers is considerable.

When you closely examine the elements of the microenvironment as part of the total Value Experience, you'll find many ways you can help customers form buying decisions; acquire, transport, store, and dispose of products; and even extend the product beyond its intended use. Pringles's cans make great organizers for pencils, pens, chopsticks, paintbrushes, and many other items found in junk drawers and garages. Egg cartons are wonderful for small jewelry and nuts, bolts, and screws. Campbell's Soup containers not only offer useful recipes, but the large plastic bottles for its ready-to-eat tomato soup make great hand weights when filled with water or sand. Unfortunately, most companies don't communicate these uses, making their packaging just packaging, or at the very least, leaving it up to the customer to figure out extended uses. With some imagination and good communication, however, the creative company can find endless possibilities.

The bottom line is every detail, no matter how small, presents an opportunity to make a product more or less valuable to the consumer. And it is our job to make sure the first is true. As we have said before, customers are why we're in business to begin with—and how we stay there. We owe it to them to deliver opening/closing mechanisms that are easy to manipulate, perforations that tear neatly, and backing that peels smoothly. We owe it to them to make instructions clear and storage and disposal efficient; if we can extend the microenvironment into other aspects of life, all the better. If doing these things for the customer is not sufficient incentive, do them for your company, because good experiences mean satisfied customers, which in the long run means more business. To that end, everyone in the microenvironment delivery chain should work together to make this important part of the Value Experience a success. That includes manufacturers, distributors, and those who rule over our next area of environment—the sellers.

The Big Picture

T RADE SHOWS, retail stores, Web sites, catalogs, lunch wagons, and even sidewalk pushcarts are all examples of the macroenvironment that supports the sale and delivery of products. On the surface these various venues may seem quite different, but in terms of experience delivery, they are really very similar. Each has the ability to delight, differentiate, and encourage loyalty and they all ultimately have only one goal—to make acquiring goods and services the best possible experience for the customer.[11] In this section we'll look at two types of macroenvironments: retail environments devoted to selling goods, and service environments where service delivery takes place.

In our consumer roles, we have all been to establishments that make consumption a pleasure. We've also been in places we couldn't wait to get out of. What makes these two experiences so different? When we ask people this question, we get a variety of answers ranging from "it was easy/confusing to find products" to "it just felt good/uncomfortable to be in the store." Whatever description they gave, all answers boiled down to three aspects of the macroenvironment that make this component a positive or negative part of the Value Experience. These three aspects are atmosphere, organization, and accessibility.[12]

Atmosphere

How does a place feel when the customer walks in the door? Is it welcoming or intimidating? Does it feel warm or sterile? Is it an atmosphere that encourages lingering or says, "Take care of business and move on"? Color, light, space, signage, décor, and even smell all contribute to an atmosphere that can, at best, be part of a great experience—or at worst, make customers leave, never to return.[13]

We are all familiar with the use of atmosphere in restaurants and entertainment venues. Bananas Foster wouldn't have been as elegant a surprise served up in the aisles of a grocery store, but set among the white-clothed tables, candlelight, and flowers of Brennan's Restaurant, it took on a special allure. Amusement parks like Disney World and grand old theaters like the Schubert in Chicago have relied on atmosphere for years to support the magic being played out on carefully constructed stage sets. In fact, the ambience that the macroenvironment creates has always been an integral part of the food and entertainment industries. But what about ordinary establishments, selling everyday products like hammers and nails, household cleaners and trash bags, potted plants and fertilizer? Can atmosphere really contribute to the customer experience when the products are mundane and the customer is just running an errand? For the answer to that question, let's visit The Home Depot, the world's largest home improvement retailer, which rakes in over $45 billion annually selling more than forty-thousand decidedly unglamorous products.[14]

Established in 1978 to serve the do-it-yourself home improvement market, The Home Depot is a model in atmospheric excellence. Deliberately designed to communicate an experience theme of no-nonsense efficiency and "guyness," it smells of sawdust and looks like a warehouse bursting with anything a home-improver might possibly need. In fact, it feels more like a giant distribution center for project materials than a place to shop. Standing in its concrete-floored, pallet-lined aisles watching the occasional forklift passing by, one fan put it this way: "It makes you feel like building a deck, remodeling the den, or just fixing something. It doesn't matter what. Ask any guy—we love [The] Home Depot. It makes us feel good."[15] Which, of course, is what the company intended.

The Home Depot's carefully crafted no-frills, you-can-tackle-anything atmosphere supports its theme of making customers feel at ease and empowered in the home improvement arena. In recent years it has broadened its offering to include design services, primarily for kitchen and bath along with turnkey remodeling. This has brought in a new, more feminine Value Group, but instead of abandoning its primary Value Group (men), it has treated the design sections of the store as small islands within the greater warehouse atmosphere. In this way The Home

Depot makes "the ladies" feel at home, without losing the atmosphere equity it worked so hard to achieve with its male customers.

This attention to atmosphere is one reason The Home Depot has become such a powerhouse. Operating in forty-eight states, Canada, Chile, Puerto Rico, and Argentina, the company expects to extend its reach from more than a thousand stores in 2001 to 2,300 stores in the Americas by the end of 2004—each one beckoning to the Tool-Time Guy it knows lurks in all of its customers.[16]

As important as this use of atmosphere is in the retail world, however, it's equally important in the service world. For any company that requires a customer to come to its location to purchase a product or use a service, atmosphere becomes a major factor in the Value Experience and should sustain an experience theme. Such basic elements as seating, décor, and proximity to rest rooms can all play an important role in how a customer feels about the overall experience. Most people are familiar with airport gate lounges and those hard plastic seats. In the days when flights departed relatively on time and customers only had to use them for a short while, these seats were probably fine. In fact, we personally don't remember registering them as a reward or a sacrifice years ago. But today, they're a real issue.

At airports like Chicago's O'Hare International, passengers are often stranded for long hours waiting to depart. Under these circumstances the seating is important, as is the rest of the macroenvironment. Lighting, air quality, and temperature all contribute to the waiting experience, which in most cases isn't a great one. To its credit, O'Hare has added more restaurants and shops to help distract passengers, but that only works for so long. The seats are still an issue when delays stretch into hours. And if you don't think seating can make a difference, just ask the patrons of Mario Tricosi's.

Chicago-based Mario Tricosi Hair Salon and Day Spas, which merged with Elizabeth Arden in 2000, opened a beautiful new salon and day spa in Vernon Hills, Illinois. This new establishment was designed from the floor up to convey the feeling of pampered care. From the minute they walked in the door, patrons knew if they turned themselves over to Mario's they would be catered to, fussed over, and leave looking like a million dollars.

Upon entering the store, customers pass through a tasteful display of pampering paraphernalia such as candles, fragrant baths salts, and creamy lotions, evoking memories of relaxing, nurturing moments in life. Just walking through this area makes you feel as though you are about to recline in the lap of luxury. Next, customers arrive at an expansive check-in counter staffed by smiling customer care representatives whose friendly and assured attitude says, "We'll take care of everything." During the check-in process, they review the services you've reserved and give you a gown to change into. Along the route to the dressing area there are strategically placed photographs of beautiful people with chic hairstyles, implying that you too can look like this at the hands of a Mario magician. By the time you're ready to settle in the waiting area, you're feeling pretty good; in fact, you're feeling great. Then bam! In the waiting area are a dozen or so cute little chairs that fit perfectly into the salon's décor. The problem is you have to be quite small to sit in them. A medium-sized woman or average-sized man feels squeezed; a large man or woman has trouble using the chairs at all. For a business whose sole purpose is to make people feel good about themselves, this is not only a gross oversight, it's inexcusable. Clearly the decorator had a field day at the customers' expense.

On the other hand, the day spa waiting room provides the ultimate pampering environment for people of all sizes. The walls are covered entirely with soft, flowing drapery. Roomy chenille-covered chairs and ottomans are cozy and welcoming. Water with lemon slices and a tasty dried fruit snack provide a light refreshment; magazines are up to date and protected by covers so they never appear tattered and worn. If services are running late, customers don't even notice, because part of the experience is waiting! This is not something many places can claim as a perk. What's more, if a patron is receiving more than one service, such as a facial and a massage, she can relax between appointments on the salon's Cleopatra-inspired lounges, surrounded by soft music and dim lights. Once again, the wait—blissfully removed from the demands of home and office—is part of the experience. Airlines, physicians, hospitals, tax preparers, auto mechanics, restaurants, and even corporate offices where customers visit can all take a few pointers from the day spa. If waiting is a good experience, people don't mind doing it.

Regardless of what you offer, ask yourself if your environment delivers welcome rewards or unnecessary sacrifices. Or, as in the case of Mario Tricosi's salon, do you score high in one area and fail in another? Also consider whether a sacrifice can be turned into a reward through environment. McDonald's wanted to attract families and kids, but a bunch of noisy youngsters running around the restaurant would drive away other patrons. This is clearly a sacrifice. However, by designing its activity centers as enclosed environments, kids can play as loudly as they want and everyone else can dine in peace. This customer-friendly move set the standard for the fast-food family experience and is the perfect lead-in to our next macroenvironment aspect—organization.

Organization

While atmosphere determines how an environment feels, organization determines how it functions. Is there adequate room to maneuver in the aisles? Are products easy to find? Is pricing and product information clear and readable? All of these factors contribute to the shopping experience. This is something McDonald's realized when it not only developed a fun atmosphere for kids and parents but also organized stores to make its environment work for all its patrons. McDonald's has always created a successful macroenvironment because it knows its customers and what they want, something our next company also discovered.

In the late 1990s Rite Aid launched an aggressive acquisition program in conjunction with the building and redesign of more than a thousand stores nationwide. These new and remodeled stores incorporated a fresh, consistent look to help revitalize the Rite Aid brand and appeal more directly to women, who make up 75 percent of its market. The success of the transformed stores was almost immediate. According to Beth Kaplan, former executive vice president of marketing, after conversion a store that was making $2 million a year jumped to $5 million a year very quickly. The key to the remodeling success, however, wasn't just a spiffy, modern look; it came from understanding its customers, how they shopped, and how best to organize the store to make shopping easier.

To help Rite Aid determine exactly how to accomplish its organizational goals, the company worked with an Atlanta design firm, Miller/

Zell, interviewing shoppers, taking bus tours of its retail facilities, and watching store videos to analyze customer behavior. What it found was that its customers are very much browsers, especially in areas like cosmetics. This information was especially helpful, because while Rite Aid is technically a "drugstore," incremental sales from front-end or nonprescription items are extremely important to profitability. In order to encourage more browsing and therefore more purchasing (studies show the longer a shopper lingers, the more she buys[17]), Rite Aid created what Kaplan calls "little refuges." "Our shopper doesn't want to have someone brushing by her," she said. "She doesn't like to be interfered with when she's shopping. If she gets bumped she moves on."[18] So it made aisles wider.

It also organized merchandise to encourage impulse buying. "We're very much in the beauty business," Kaplan said. That's why when you enter a newer Rite Aid store, one of the first things you see is an extensive cosmetics department where one section of products flows into the next. One Rite Aid customer described it as an "unfolding of self-nurturing products" that draws her in every time she goes to the pharmacy to pick up a prescription. "I usually end up buying something extra," she says.[19] Which of course means the Rite Aid plan is working.

To make other areas easy to find, the stores also feature a "main drive aisle" that runs diagonally through the store and gives a preview of other key departments. Eighty percent of Rite Aid's customers travel the main drive aisle, states Kaplan. This not only helps the customer find products, but also makes it easier for the store to showcase new products and encourage those impulse sales.

In the years following its acquisition and remodeling push, Rite Aid experienced financial difficulties, due not to experience issues but to business problems—primarily inventory shortages and a reduced and erratic advertising program. Currently in turn-around mode, however, it is making more money with fewer stores and still shows double-digit sales increases in remodeled locations.[20]

Accessibility

As important as good organization is to both a business and its customers, equally important is being able to access the product once it's been found. Like organization, accessibility is one of those experience factors that falls under the "common sense" heading. Why would a company sell products a customer can't get to? Yet consistently we find products out of reach, especially in the self-service world of grocery stores, discount outlets, and specialty retailers. Unless a store has an associate in every aisle, and we know that's not the case, a customer should never have to find someone to retrieve a product. Customers don't like it. Ask them. We did.

In chapter 3 we related just such an incident with the OXO can opener. Once we recovered from the annoyance of not being able to reach the sought-after can opener, we decided to find out if we were the only ones this bothered. Over the course of two days, we conducted fifty exit interviews outside a Bed, Bath & Beyond store.[21] When asked what they liked about shopping at the store, 57 percent cited product selection as number one. On the other hand, when asked what they would improve about the store, 33 percent mentioned "out of reach" products. So what's a store to do when people want selection but also want accessibility? The answer might be easier than you think.

Once we knew we were not the only ones who were frustrated by inaccessible products in certain areas of Bed, Bath & Beyond, we decided to see how the store might be able to solve the problem without destroying its entire retail model. Over the next half-hour we paced and measured and counted. Finally we spotted the problem. The rows were going the wrong way. All of the products were hung in horizontal rows— a row of pizza cutters, a row of bottle openers, a row of potato peelers. The more products, the more rows, and before long a shopper's height determined what items he or she might reasonably access.

By our calculations, however, if you took the same number of products and organized them in vertical columns instead, customer height would no longer be an issue. It appears that just by reorganizing the way the products are displayed, every single customer could reach every single OXO product. Michael Jordan and Martin Short could stand side by side and each would have an OXO can opener at eye level. The customer has a good experience, the store keeps its wall of utensils, and OXO makes a sale.

It would be nice if all issues of atmosphere, organization, and access were this simple to solve, and we know of course they're not. But whether the challenge is simple or complex, the solution always begins with customers. When they come to the marketplace, what delights or dismays them? How does the experience leave them feeling? What can you do to make it better? It doesn't matter whether you own the macroenvironment you're selling in or not. If you don't and it is not providing the best experience for your customers, work with your outlet to remedy the situation. If you do own the space, imagine how pleased your customers and suppliers will be if you take the initiative yourself. When you start with the customer your chances of ending with a sale and repeat business are that much greater—even if catering to the shopper means you have to go to them.

Indeed, sometimes asking customers to come to you doesn't work as well as going to them. This is often true in commercial settings where decision makers want to see products, but time to "go shopping" is difficult to find. Back in the 1980s, American Edwards Labs, a medical equipment company, faced this challenge when trying to schedule doctors to view a demonstration of the first ambulatory Holter monitor.[22] The device consisted of two parts. A small recorder with EKG leads was worn by patients to allow doctors to view heart activity during the course of a day, while a large scanner read the tapes and analyzed them for irregular heartbeats. The small part of the device could easily be carried to the doctor's location, but the larger piece was another matter. Because of this size constraint, American Edwards initially considered only showing samples of the readouts, but in order to evaluate the new equipment accurately, a doctor needed to see it in action.

To facilitate the optimum demonstration of the product, the company provided each salesman with a custom van, which included a fully functional scanner, a refrigerator for refreshments, chairs, and a phone for the doctor to use in case he or she was paged. The salesman would pull into a hospital parking lot, collect the doctor, and demo the equipment. The van was a creative use of the macroenvironment that reduced the sales call time for both the company and the customer while giving the doctor all the information needed to properly evaluate the new technology. Thinking out of the box like this is often required to bring real value to the customer.

That statement has probably never been truer than it is today. Research shows that people feel as though they have less time, more demands on their time, and more companies trying to sell them goods and services than ever before. To cut through the clutter and provide people with offerings that support their lives, we need to learn as much as we can about our customers. In turn they will give us the direction we need to truly become customer-centric. It's a symbiotic relationship of give and take that is important to nurture in every aspect of environment—even when that environment is virtual.

The Web Factor

TECHNICALLY part of the macroenvironment, the Internet has created an entirely new marketplace. But whether your macroenvironment is a brick-and-mortar location, a virtual address, or a combination of the two, the principles of atmosphere, organization, and accessibility still apply. Let's take a quick look at how each can be used to make the Internet marketplace a more customer-friendly experience.

Web Atmosphere

Whether a Web site is selling products or supporting a company or brand, the atmosphere, or look and feel, of a site is just as important online as it is in the concrete world. From the home page, which is the virtual store's front door or lobby, to its various departments, a Web site's atmosphere should communicate an experience theme and make customers feel welcome and comfortable.

The Home Depot carries its theme of no-nonsense efficiency and "guyness" to its Web site by using masculine colors and straightforward, task-oriented section titles like "Fix It," "Build It," and "Install It." As a counterpart to the stores' wide aisles, the site features pages that are roomy and not overcrowded with pictures or links so it's easy to "browse." You even see a few friendly faces, with virtual helpers dressed in familiar Home Depot aprons appearing on many pages. The company hasn't figured out how to deliver the sawdust smell, but when it does, we're sure that fresh-hewn aroma will be part of the experience as well. When you visit The Home Depot Web site, you feel as though you've just cruised the aisles of your local store because the company has done such a credible job with its Web atmosphere.

Web Organization

Organization in a virtual marketplace is perhaps even more important than it is in a real one. At least in a store you can ask for help. Online you're usually on your own. For that reason it is critical for a Web site to have clear menu bars, intuitive navigation, and easy movement between pages. Nothing is more maddening than to dig down several layers to access information only to find you've taken a wrong turn and can't find your way back.

One of our favorite sites for clean, understandable, customer-friendly organization is butterball.com. A perfect example of how the Internet can be used to enhance value during the integrate stage, it offers preparation tips, recipes, and fun turkey facts as well as seasonal stories about turkey traditions. Since the site went live in 1995, it has helped over five million people make selecting, thawing, and cooking turkey easier.

Key to its success is a search engine and navigation tools that make finding information simple. For instance, you can search for recipes by title if you are coming back to find an old favorite or by criteria such as lifestyle. The lifestyle selection is particularly interesting, with categories such as "On the Patio," "Quick & Easy," and "Comfort Food." When you click into a section, recipes for main dishes as well as soups, side dishes, and sandwiches are listed. And not every recipe uses turkey; there are chicken dishes as well as vegetable and dessert ideas, making the site more valuable than it would be with a turkey-only focus. Also, when you click on an individual recipe, a popup window appears, allowing you to either jot down the instructions or print them in a format that lends itself well to storing in a notebook. There's even room for notes. When you're done, you simply close the window and you're still on the recipe selection page. This feature makes it easy to access multiple dishes without excessive navigation.

Whether the purpose of a Web site is commerce, support, communications, or information, organization is one of the most important elements in the online customer's experience. Don't underestimate its ability
to deliver extraordinary rewards or intolerable sacrifices.

Web Accessibility

Accessibility has a slightly different meaning in a Web environment
than it does in a brick-and-mortar marketplace. Whereas in a physical
space we talked about making products easy to locate and retrieve in cy-
berspace you may have the added challenge of finding the site itself and
retrieval usually comes in the form of a shopping cart or downloads.
Both of these issues can greatly affect the experience a customer has
with a Web site, primarily during discover and acquire stages.

There are various ways to make sure people can discover your Web
site, and most of them are pretty simple. Every company with a Web
presence should make sure that it is registered with search engines and
that those registrations are refreshed at least quarterly. Your Webmaster
can develop metatags and key words, those phrases and words your potential customers type to find information by topic or company. Knowing your Value Groups and what they are likely to key in is particularly
helpful here. Web addresses should also be included on all physical materials such as ads, brochures, and store displays. Pumpkin Masters, a
Denver-based company that developed a simple and safe method for
kids to carve intricate patterns on pumpkins, markets its carving kits
through traditional retailers. It also offers contests, carving tips, and a
free pattern online. Unfortunately, the company doesn't mention its
Web site on its product packaging. This is a missed opportunity to send
customers to Pumpkin Masters' virtual world, where it might extend the
customer experience much as Butterball has done with its Web site.
Unfortunately, the site also suffers from sins of omission—it does not
include a list of retail outlets, so people who stumble across the Web
site have no way to locate the product in a store.

Once people find a site, it should be easy to both retrieve information and make purchases. These steps are primarily technical issues, so

we won't go into too much detail here. Suffice it to say, pages should load quickly and transactions occur smoothly, requiring minimal effort from the customer. Whenever possible, personalize interactions with customers and give them choices. One of the reasons the Internet emerged as a major macroenvironment is the level of control and accessibility it affords today's consumer; it can add a great deal of value when used properly.

Circuit City does an excellent job of selling products on its Web site while also supporting the brick-and-mortar environment, but we particularly appreciate an accessibility feature it pioneered several years ago. Once a product is selected, customers have three choices: purchase the product online and have it shipped, purchase online and pick it up at their nearest Circuit City location, or check inventory of an item and then go to a store to buy it. The customer can also return online purchases to a store. These options make shopping with Circuit City easy and accessible any time of the day or night. As the company continues to open new stores (which sport a fresh, well-organized redesign), we hope more shoppers will discover the value Circuit City delivers through this component.

How to Be Environmentally Friendly

As with product and service, it is virtually impossible to cover all the elements of environment that affect an offering's value. In the category of microenvironments alone, there are hundreds of details to address and each one has the power to enhance or detract from an experience. As a company, you need to put your microenvironment under a microscope, so to speak, and examine it for flaws in value delivery just as you do your product. You might form an interdepartmental committee to serve as a "microenvironment protection agency." After identifying the rewards and sacrifices of your current microenvironment, the group could set guidelines to make sure this important component is delivering the experience your customers expect. Even small changes in this area can add significant value from the customer's perspective.

Macroenvironments can be more challenging if a company does not own the environment in which its product is sold or delivered. In these circumstances, it is important to solicit the support of your distribution channel and educate them about the Value Experience you are trying to deliver. Whether manufacturer, retailer, or service provider, you should form a group of people from various levels of the company to interact as customers do within your macroenvironments. What experiences do the atmosphere, organization, and accessibility of the environment deliver? What are the rewards and sacrifices customers encounter and at what stage does each occur? Use the experience event matrix (chapter 2) to gauge the impact of each event on value and then formulate a plan to eliminate sacrifices or even turn those sacrifices into rewards, just as Pepsi did with its packaging. When you give environment the same attention you devote to product and service, you're only one step away from a true Value Experience.

PRICELESS ROADMAP—CHAPTER 6

> ➤ Identify the type of environment, macro or micro, that is appropriate to your business and where you think you can have the greatest impact on the Value Experience.

> ➤ Identify the experience events involving interaction between customer and environment and in which stage of the EEP they occur.

> ➤ Identify opportunities to increase a reward, eliminate a sacrifice, or turn a sacrifice into a reward.

CHAPTER seven

The Gift

FROM THE CUSTOMER WITH LOVE

W HEN PROCTER & GAMBLE OPENED ITS CUSTOMER service lines more than fifty years ago, its primary objective was to solve consumer problems and provide value-added services. As it turned out, however, taking care of customers' immediate needs wasn't the only advantage of this program. In addition to answering questions about getting the stains out of little Johnny's baseball uniform or baking brownies at high altitudes, the service proved to be an effective tool for revealing customer habits and preferences, even if the company didn't know it at the time.

During the 1960s, for instance, while solving customers' laundry problems, the consumer products giant found that the average household's weekly laundry increased from 6.4 to 7.6 loads. It also discovered that the average wash temperature dropped 15 degrees. Were Americans wearing more clothes than before? Was a fuel conservation trend invading the laundry room? After digging a little further, the company found it wasn't consumer habits that were changing, but what they were washing. Innovations in the textile industry had resulted in a rash of new synthetic fabrics such as polyester. These new materials required closer sorting—thus more loads—and a wider range of water temperature settings. As a result of these findings, the company created All-Temperature Cheer laundry detergent. The washing public loved it and Cheer is still one of the company's most popular brands. From our perspective, though, the real story isn't laundry ease, but the customer who gave the company a tremendous gift. This gift, disguised as conversations and complaints, was insight. By sharing their laundry experiences with Procter & Gamble, the customer gave the company exactly the vision it needed to develop a sure hit.[1]

Every day customers give businesses similar gifts. Through a variety of avenues they reveal their thoughts and feelings, unveil their values, and communicate the rewards and sacrifices of their experiences. In this final chapter we'll see how to access these gifts and use them to give the customer something in return—a Value Experience. We'll begin by looking at traditional forms of information and what they tell us about consumers. This information is both objective and quantifiable and provides us with a starting point for a more refined view of consumers. Next we'll examine subjective information, which tells us why consumers make purchases. This leads to a better understanding of their values. Finally, we'll look at insight. This is the customer's own priceless offering, a gift that offers us a glimpse into the future. Properly used, it allows us to reap the rewards of focusing first and always on our most valuable asset—our customers. But before we can do this, we need to know more about them.

What's Up

WHETHER CUSTOMERS are aware of it or not, they are constantly providing important information about themselves. This information often comes in the form of historical data, such as buying frequency and dollars spent; customer feedback via surveys, comments, complaints, or questions; and market research, which provides demographic information, patterns of behavior, preferences, and so on.

As businesspeople, we're accustomed to gathering and using this type of information. In fact, information gathering and research has become so sophisticated that we can pinpoint very fine details about our customers. For instance, Nissan Design International tested more than ninety samples of leather to find three that U.S. noses favored for their Infinity J-30.[2] This allowed the company to provide a pleasant sensory experience for a very specific market. The fast-food industry knows that people between the ages of thirteen and twenty-four are the most frequent patrons of its restaurants, so it tailors products and marketing to this market segment.[3] Most grocery stores today track purchases through identification cards, allowing them to create special promotions based on buying patterns. These are all creditable uses of information that have helped businesses more closely target what people want. We believe, however, that even more can be done with information if we tweak the focus to recognize not just what people want or prefer, but what they value. First USA Bank is a good example of how this focus on value can work for everyone.

For years Visa and MasterCard, along with their respective bank outlets, have been matching wits trying to attract consumers to their credit cards. But with so many competitors playing the interest rate game, it was hard to cut through the clutter. Finally, unwilling to yield to constant price pressure, First USA was determined to find a way to make a credit card more than a piece of plastic. Like most of us, the company began with what it already knew: People needed a credit card. It's hard to function in today's world without one. It also knew that people expected low rates and didn't care which card they used as long as the rate was low.

Looking for a fresh approach to product development, First USA began by viewing the customer not merely as a credit card user, but as a whole person engaged in many life experiences. With this new perspective as its focus, the company looked for a different kind of information. What were people's interests? What groups did they belong to? What did they read? Before long it found that among the million of credit card users, there were sports lovers, pet lovers, and art lovers. Others were proud to show their association with political parties, charities, and professional organizations. There were even those who liked to declare their attachment to magazines like *Reader's Digest* and *National Geographic*. Once it recognized the importance people placed on these relationships, it not only knew what consumers wanted, it knew what very specific groups valued. Today, any bank will tell you that an affinity card holder is the most loyal because the card with the horses, the Chicago Bulls, or the Christian symbol on it isn't just a card. It represents an important part of someone's life—a part he or she values enough to see it encased in plastic.

As a result of their discovery, First USA has more than 750 different credit offerings, each presenting a different combination of variables such as interest rate, annual fees, and add-on features based on each Value Group's individual needs.[4] Each time a company identifies a Value Group it can begin to uncover the information needed to refine product offerings and even redirect an enterprise to deliver a better Value Experience. A case in point is Taco Bell.

In the late 1980s a struggling Taco Bell conducted a refined study of its customer base to see if it could more clearly identify its best customers. Up until this time Taco Bell operated solely as a generic mass-marketer. Based on the broad demographic and psychographic categories favored by most fast-food organizations, its target market was loosely identified as young people between the ages of thirteen and twenty-four who were high-frequency fast-food users, or HFFFUs. While this was a start, this information wasn't enough to tell Taco Bell what it was doing right or wrong. It needed more.

Starting with the broad HFFFU market, Taco Bell identified three key segments—people who visited Taco Bell at least once a week, people who visited Taco Bell as little as once a month, and people who never patronized Taco Bell because they don't like Mexican food. Focusing on the people who not only liked Mexican food but also liked Taco Bell, it attempted to find out what made these people tick. What it found were two distinct Value Groups: "penny-pinchers" and "speed freaks."

The first group was identified as eighteen- to twenty-four-year-olds who use Taco Bell frequently but narrowly, spending as little as possible while buying three to four items from the lowest-priced offerings on the menu. What it deduced from this behavior is that while these customers liked variety, price really was first on their list. The second group was made up of harried, two-income couples and families who wanted quick, hassle-free meals that tasted good time after time, store after store. This group was more interested in process than prices, and although these customers also appreciated variety, good and fast were more important qualities.

Ironically, what both groups wanted, good and cheap and good and fast, had nothing to do with the company's existing business development strategy. Believing a more elaborate, widely varied menu would attract more people, the company had continually been adding high-priced items to the menu. In other words, it was focusing on product and not customer. The strategy wasn't working and now it knew why. When all the information was analyzed, it found these two primary Value Groups represented 70 percent of their volume—*70 percent*—and neither group was particularly interested in a continually revised, high-priced menu. Clearly it was time for a change.

Once Taco Bell had a more accurate picture of who its best customers were, it made the decision to focus exclusively on leveraging those Value Groups—not an easy decision. As simple as it sounds, taking this path meant redefining its business concept and reengineering core processes to limit the sacrifices and increase the rewards for both groups. To do this, the company first created the FACT concept (fast food Fast, orders Accurate, in a Clean environment at the right Temperature). This action was followed by a streamlined menu and a major speed-of-service program that transformed operations from an on-demand approach to an inventory approach. This initiative resulted in a 54 percent peak-hour capacity increase and a 71 percent reduction in waiting time. This helped improve the acquire stage for both groups, but particularly addressed the speed freaks' need for efficiency.

To attract new customers and better serve existing ones, the company also deemphasized store-based production and invested in multiple channels of distribution such as kiosks, carts, and counters in places like malls, college cafeterias, airports, and even gas stations. As we discussed in the chapter on environment, sometimes you have to go to the people. This further enhanced the acquire stage by adding increased convenience to the efficiency of earlier improvements. It didn't forget the penny-pinchers either. To cater to its most active Value Group, the company shifted its core menu offerings from higher-priced selections to 59-cent, 79-cent, and 99-cent items. In fact, in 1988 Taco Bell reduced its pricing to 25 percent below what it had been in 1982. By adding greater choice within this Value Group's price range, it increased value.

The result of this focus on serving its Value Groups was extraordinary growth. Sales increased from $1.6 billion in 1988 to $3.9 billion in 1993. Earnings rose from $82 million in 1988 to $253 million in 1993. In 1994 the company's sales totaled $4.5 billion and earnings topped $273 million.[5] Clearly, having the right information on which to base decisions paid off in the long run.

We Knew That!

WHAT MAKES TACO BELL one of our favorite experience success stories is that it not only gathered the right information, it made a genuine effort to comprehend what its customers wanted in terms of both value and the dining experience. Too often companies stop short of taking information to this next step, which we define as understanding.

While information is very much focused on "what" and "who," understanding is more about "why." For example, a survey that asks customers how they heard about you provides a "what"—in this case, which avenue of promotion or contact was most effective. But if you asked the same customers why they selected your product, you would have understanding as well as information. Both are necessary pieces of the puzzle.

When the Horse Industry Alliance (HIA) surveyed sixty thousand Americans about their interest in riding, it identified four distinct Value Groups: those who rode for recreation, rode for the thrill of competition, owned horses primarily for business, and people who didn't ride but had an affinity for horses.[6] When it looked more closely at those who chose riding as their preferred form of recreation, it found that riding helped relieve stress, allowed them to feel connected with nature, and provided a good source of exercise without the usual tedium of a workout. On the value model this would translate to nurturing and spiritual connection. For the multibillion dollar horse industry, whose largest segment is the recreational rider, knowing this "why" not only helps breed and sport associations tailor programs to better serve this Value Group, but allows them to more closely target messages to reach, for instance, stressed-out executive women and outdoor enthusiasts.

Understanding why people are attracted to one product over another is obviously something every company wants and needs to know. Not only can this information help a business eliminate wasted time and money developing products and features people don't really want (Microsoft's annoying talking paper clip comes to mind), it also helps target new offerings. Armed with an understanding of the emotional and spiritual connection a large segment of the population had for horses, HIA convinced MBNA to launch a Visa affinity credit card for the general public, featuring horses. In its first year, the card far exceeded expectations for acceptance.[7] Others too have found that gaining a clear understanding of their Value Groups early in the product design stage can take a great deal of the risk out of new product development. Just ask Mercedes-Benz.

By the late 1990s nearly every car manufacturer offered a sports utility vehicle (SUV). In addition to the "working man" nameplates like Ford and Chevy, luxury lines such as Cadillac, Lexus, Infiniti, and Lincoln also had their own versions of the popular truck already out or on the way. It was only a matter of time before Mercedes would have to follow suit or seriously risk losing luxury market share.[8] Targeting the United States as its primary geographic market, Mercedes' parent company, DaimlerChrysler, dove into the project with both feet. Building a new factory in Tuscaloosa, Alabama, and instituting a new production process, it gave the new entry—dubbed an All Activity Vehicle (AAV)—every operational opportunity to compete. Now it was up to the product design engineers and the marketers to determine just what customers wanted in the new vehicle.

There are always risks in launching a new product, but with the pressures of a recently built plant, tough competition, and a slowing SUV market, the pressure to get the new Mercedes right was tremendous. In order to reduce risk as much as possible, Mercedes launched an aggressive initiative to understand what customers would respond to. Direct mail targeted at seven hundred thousand potential customers not only created awareness of the upcoming new vehicle, but also included a survey on desired features of a future M-Class vehicle. This gathered information that told Mercedes what people were looking for. Follow-up communications and public relations campaigns yielded a more refined database of one hundred thousand highly desirable customers who indicated a serious interest in a new vehicle. This gave Mercedes a base to begin building its Value Groups.

From these contacts Mercedes learned that even though prospective buyers were charmed by the rugged image conjured up by this type of vehicle, they still expected comfort and performance. After all, it was a Mercedes. The researchers also found that safety was important to this group, especially current Mercedes owners, who would initially be the primary target for the new vehicle. In addition, the data gathered indicated that if Mercedes kept the cost around $35,000, the M-Class AAV would play very well as a second family vehicle, primarily for women in the United States. At this price point the company believed it might also have a shot at a younger market in Europe. This group was not currently made up of Mercedes owners, but they had very specific context needs Mercedes thought it could address.

"In the USA, it has more to do with lifestyle and with what a successful family wants to be seen driving," commented Carsten Bauer, M-Class product manager. "In Europe, the market is less clear. There is purpose behind their decision. For example, they use such vehicles to go to their cottages in the mountains or to tow a boat or a horse box, or to go hunting."[9] These two different Value Groups presented two different types of challenges to the company. The first group clearly wanted a vehicle that appealed to a more emotional set of values such as comfort, status, and self-esteem with a bit of adventurous freedom thrown in, while the Europeans were looking for more intellectually focused values such as performance and design excellence. He also noted that while more women than men would be driving the vehicle in the United States, the exact opposite would be true in Europe.

So, faced with two different Value Groups, the company did the only thing it could. It designed the new vehicle to satisfy both. Judging correctly that the luxury crowd wouldn't mind owning a great performance vehicle and the performance fans wouldn't turn down a little comfort, the M-Class Mercedes was so enthusiastically received that in its first year on the market, buyers waited as long as seven months to get one.

But as we all know, it takes more than a great product to produce sales. People have to know it's there, and Mercedes did an exceptionally good job in the discover stage. During the launch of the M-Class it not only announced the new vehicle's arrival; it let people know the automaker understood the value customers were looking for. This revelation began with its own description of the vehicle:

> *Widely acclaimed for its perfect combination of off- and on-road abilities, the M-Class is a new breed of off-roader that challenges convention. It gives perfect expression to two different characters—elegance and* sportiness—*in one body shell without sacrificing their individuality.*
>
> *It is seldom that one is simultaneously swept away by a vehicle's rugged appeal, uncompromising quality, air of sophisticated defiance and sheer sense of purpose.*[10]

This is a beautifully crafted Value Experience statement. It identifies both Value Groups, it communicates the key values, and it paints a picture that puts the customer right into the experience of owning, driving, enjoying, and appreciating the Mercedes M-Class. This overall message was then segmented by individual values that were highlighted in a series of commercials. One ad featured a baby appearing to sing the praises of his father who has securely fastened him in the back seat of an M-Class. This addressed the safety factor. Another showed a child building a house of cards in the back seat while a boy passes a hot cup of tea to his grandmother, all without incident. This one covered comfort and that famous smooth Mercedes ride. A third was designed to appeal to the baby boomers' sense of nostalgia (they had been identified as a key market) as well as create an association for the vehicle with a class act. This spot spoke to the status and self-esteem values. The company did this by using digitally doctored film of Ed Sullivan, who was known for introducing hot new stars on his hit television program. In the ad Sullivan appears, rubbing his hands together while saying, "Headlining tonight's really big show, is the Mercedes-Benz M-Class."[11] The car shows off its features on a stage designed to resemble the Sullivan set of past decades. Sullivan applauds, laughs, and comments on what he sees. The clear association the ad made with first-class acts like Elvis Presley and the Beatles, who also shared the Sullivan stage at one time, was very effective.

The combination of the right vehicle marketed with the right message was so successful that Mercedes-Benz sold 7,200 of the vehicles almost immediately. Based on these early sales, the company upped its initial production estimates from 33,000 units to 40,000 units in the United States. It missed that estimate too—coming in nearly 50 percent higher in its inaugural year. The following year sales rose 33 percent, and in January 2001 the Tuscaloosa plant celebrated the roll-off of the two-hundred and fifty thousandth M-Class AAV—a full year ahead of schedule. With no signs of slowing, the company has expanded its U.S. plant and added M-Class production at the Daimler-Puch plant in Graz, Austria, primarily to handle increased demand in Europe.

What we can learn from both the M-Class and the Taco Bell success we discussed earlier is that determining what the customer values and then dedicating the company to delivering those values reaps great dividends for everyone. The customer receives a Value Experience and the company, along with all those involved in the making and delivering of the product, grows. In addition, when customers know you understand them, they are more likely to stay with you. By one account, Mercedes' customer loyalty increased by nearly ten percentage points in the first three months of the 1998 model year, due in large part to the M-Class. And while, as expected, current owners of Mercedes represented 70 percent of initial M-Class buyers, that percentage has since dropped to 50 percent as the vehicle attracts a growing number of first-time Mercedes owners.

What could your company do armed with a clearer understanding of the Value Experience your customers are looking for? Could you streamline operations and better target product offerings, as did Taco Bell? Like Mercedes-Benz, could you reduce some of the risk of launching a new product? Or maybe you could do a better job of meeting customer expectations while limiting sacrifice and increasing rewards.

Canadian Pacific Hotels (CPH), with twenty-seven properties ranging from the elegant Royal York in Toronto to the Rocky Mountains' Banff

Springs Hotel, wanted to target a new audience to help increase business. Already quite successful in the convention, meeting, and corporate group markets, the hotel chain set its sites on the individual business traveler, or what Brian Richardson, vice president of marketing for CPH, called "the most discerning and demanding customers in the history of mankind."[12] Having gathered all the industry data available, which included information such as frequency, average length of stay, services used, and so forth, it still felt it did not have a grip on what customer expectations were for a preferred place to stay while traveling on business. So the company turned to the customer for answers. What it found was a group of individuals with very different and personal ideas about what constituted a good hotel experience. Everyone of course wants basics such as good service and a clean room. But when asked what would make their experience truly extraordinary, the answers were all over the map. Despite this seeming lack of direction, the company was determined to attract this highly lucrative customer. Taking the challenge in hand, CPH embarked on a mission to meet as many individual quirks and preferences as its customers could produce.

The hotel chain began catering to the individuality of the customer by instituting a frequent guest club, which promised that the hotel would move heaven and earth to meet a member's every wish. Whether it was a king-sized bed, a room on a high floor, or Mountain Dew in the minibar, it was determined to meet these requests at every single stay at any of the twenty-seven CPH properties.

Staying within the context of the business trip, the company next mapped out every aspect of the guest experience. From pulling up at the hotel to accepting the car keys from the valet at the end of the stay, each event—and there were dozens of them—was identified. The company then prescribed the highest level of service for each event, based on what customers said they expected. This is an important distinction. The metrics for level of service were set by the customer, not the company. It recognized that only the customer could set these expectations. From there the company determined what products or services were needed to make it all happen—not just once or in one location, but consistently across the enterprise. Richardson admits this was not always easy. "Our bias had been toward serving groups," he said, "so there was significant cultural change." The skills needed to gather a busload of convention-eers together and send them off to the airport on time are very different from those needed to deal with a CEO who wants an extra-large bathrobe, a copy of the *Financial Times,* and a six-pack of chilled water in his room. In time it became clear that the company's commitment to this new Value Group meant the management structure had to change.

At each hotel a champion was appointed and given broad cross-functional authority to see that staff lived up to the customers' expectations. The company also implemented a new technology to enable better tracking and communication among hotels in the chain. The effort paid off in short order. While the Canadian business travel market increased just 3 percent overall, CPH's numbers jumped 16 percent, and that was without adding new properties to the chain. Analysis of the numbers revealed that the growth could be traced to the fact that a full quarter of the frequent guest club members stopped spending money with competitors. Instead, they remained loyal to the one who gave them what they valued most—being treated like an individual and very special guest.[13]

Amazing what a little understanding can do. It allows you to deliver exactly and only what customers want; it allows you to create new products that meet customer needs and speak to their values as if they were sitting with you at the drawing table. Finally, it allows you to foster loyalty that brings more stability to your business than anything else you can do. But as important as understanding is, it's not the last gift the customer contributes to the Value Experience. The ultimate contribution from the customer is insight.

The Brightest Bulb in the Bunch

O NE MIGHT ARGUE that understanding is a very close cousin to insight, and one would be right. As Taco Bell, Mercedes, and Canadian Pacific Hotels gathered information and talked with customers, they were able to form an understanding of their Value Groups and what the companies needed to do to deliver a Value Experience. We know this approach works and delivers great results for everyone. But what if we could take it one step further? What if we could not only see what has already happened (information) and see why it happened (understanding), but also predict what will happen in the future? If we could conjure up this vision with some reliability, wouldn't it be remarkable? It actually can be done if you move beyond what and why to "what if." That's the role of insight—to help us look at what is and imagine what can be. Consider the case of Hewlett-Packard and the surgeon.[14]

Wanting to know more about her customers' environment, a Hewlett-Packard product developer sat in an operating room observing surgeons at work. During one operation the surgeon was guiding his scalpel by watching the patient's body and his hands on a TV monitor. Occasionally a nurse would walk in front of the monitor, briefly blocking the doctor's view. This didn't seem to bother anyone; it was just the way it was, an acceptable sacrifice, so to speak. But our curious observer made a note of the event and over time began to wonder what her company could do about it. The answer turned out to be a lightweight helmet that could suspend the video images a few inches from the surgeon's eyes. This not only eliminated the sacrifice caused by interruptions, it added a reward. By increasing accuracy, the new product provided an all-around safer instrument for doctor and patient. Doctors would never have asked for this innovation because they didn't know it was possible. This is the real benefit of insight—to be able to glean from customers what they want and need even if they are unable to articulate their desires. There are various ways to gain this insight. Procter & Gamble used a hot line and conversations with customers to gain insight into the everyday lives of homemakers. This method is often effective when a large customer base is available to work from. Another method we particularly like is the one Hewlett-Packard used—observation. Although observation is more time- and labor-intensive, it puts you closer to the customer and allows you to interact in a more personal way. It also allows the customer to participate more fully in cocreating the Value Experience.

In an article entitled "Spark Innovation Through Empathic De-sign," two Harvard Business School professors, Dorothy Leonard and Jeffrey F. Rayport, explore observation and its role in product innova-tion. "When a product or service is well understood," they explain, "traditional marketing science provides amazingly sophisticated ways to gain useful information from potential customers and influence their purchasing decisions."[15] The same rationale applies to known technologies. Because people understood the concept and technology behind the compact disc for music, it wasn't a stretch for them to imagine how it could be applied to movies. So when researchers asked how a customer would feel about buying movies that came on a com-pact disc, she could answer.

But what if a concept is so new that customers can't imagine it? Or, more commonly, what if customers are so accustomed to "what is" that they can't imagine "what if?" In both of these cases, customers may not be able to tell us what they want, think, or feel, but we can gain insight into what they might value by watching them in their own world. A widely told story about the powers of observation in bringing new tech-nology to the marketplace occurred in 1915. According to business lore, a man named David Sarnoff was observing families gathered in their liv-ing rooms after supper. Watching them, it occurred to him that the radio, then used only to transmit Morse code, might be handy for bringing news, music, and baseball to America's homes. The typical person didn't know anything about radio waves or what they could transmit, so he re-ally couldn't articulate how swell this little miracle might be. Sarnoff, however, put two and two together for him, and the result revolutionized American life.[16]

This use of informed observers, people who understand the capabil-ities of the organization (and, we would add, consumer values as well), has tremendous potential for all businesses regardless of size or offering. Instead of spending time on innovations customers *might* want you could actually work on products or improvements they *will* want. When Nissan Design's president, Jerry Hirshberg, was driving down the street one day, he noticed a couple on the side of the road trying to cram a piece of furniture into their minivan. When he stopped to talk, they told him they had purchased the van for just such a purpose, but in order to take advantage of the cargo space, they had to remove the seats. Eventually this chance meeting led to the idea for using six-foot runners so the van's backseat could fold up, quickly freeing the cargo space.[17]

What we find interesting about this story is not so much that Hirshberg happened on the struggling family, but that he took the opportunity to learn from them. As part of the business community, we observe customers interacting with products, services, and environments in the real world all the time. What's more, we interact with all three in the real world ourselves. And yet very few of us in our employee lives are encouraged to bring our observations about those experiences with us to work. Most companies have a rich resource of observers right under their noses. What have your employees seen, overheard, or experienced themselves? In fact, how many of your employees are your customers, too? Probably quite a few, but companies seldom take advantage of this highly available pool of insight.

When companies do turn to the customer for insight, however, they begin to see the company and its products through new eyes and with a clearer vision of what actually is—not what they think or even want it to be. How many of you have ever used a shop vacuum—the barrel-shaped type on wheels whose top-mounted motor has a hose protruding next to it? Just about every handyman owns one, and just about every handyman uses the hose to pull the vacuum across the floor. Of course, the first page of the manual tells you not to do this because it will probably tip over from the weight of the motor. Naturally, nearly every user has tipped one over and spilled the contents onto the floor. But no matter, we all continue to pull on the hose because that's the easiest way to move the vacuum while in use.

After years of spilled sawdust, Sears finally recognized this experience disconnect and decided to take the customer's lead. The Sears Craftsman Low Profile Wet/Dry Vacuum has a lower center of gravity, and the hose attaches below the motor. As a result, the vacuum doesn't easily tip over, even when pulled by the hose. We're glad Sears redesigned the product to fit actual use, but one has to wonder what took so long. Didn't anyone who worked for Sears use a ShopVac? Probably many did, but if you don't ask, they won't tell—not because they don't want to, but because they don't know to.

This is often the case with insight. By its very nature it requires looking beyond the obvious because people can't always articulate what creates value in a product. When consultants for Kimberly-Clark visited customers to gauge the appeal of pull-on diapers for toddlers, it discovered that parents didn't consider diapers a disposable product as the company thought, but an article of clothing.[18] This discovery gave the product a whole new dimension in terms of looks as well as pricing, but more important, it uncovered hidden value.

By observing and then talking to parents, the company learned that the adults saw pull-on diapers as a positive step toward more mature behavior and very useful in the potty-training process. Putting on "big-boy pants" was an emotional as well as practical step in the growing-up process for parent and child. Suddenly Kimberly-Clark wasn't dealing with a different-shaped diaper, but a right of passage that to moms everywhere was priceless. Understanding the importance of this message, *given to them by the customer,* the company launched Huggies Pull-Ups with an "I'm a big kid now" theme. It rolled out nationally in 1991, catching the competition with its diapers down to the tune of $400 million in annual product sales. All because Kimberly-Clark observed, listened to, and understood the customer.

We began this book asking why the MasterCard commercial couldn't be true and everything we buy with it lead to something priceless. The truth is, with effort, dedication, and the customer by your side, the products you offer can lead to something priceless—the Value Experience. Our job has been to point the way and outline the steps to get you started on the right path. We don't pretend it will be easy. For many companies, focusing on the Value Experience will require cultural, organizational, and functional transformation from company-centric to customer-centric. But even if you start small, one positive step forward will lead to another.

Begin by appointing a team to learn about value and the role it plays in your customers' lives. From there you can identify your Value Groups. Next evaluate your products and map what you believe they offer today in terms of the attributes listed on the Value Model. Then walk through the Experience Engagement Process with your customers and identify the experience events they encounter. By doing this you can identify the rewards and sacrifices they receive and revise the value profile of your offerings based on their experiences. Armed with this view of your business and your products, focus on a component or, better still, on a single stage, eliminating sacrifices and increasing the rewards surrounding it. By starting small and experiencing success, it will make it easer to continue the process until you reach your goal of delivering a complete Value Experience. It won't happen overnight. But it is possible, as countless companies have already proven.

Those companies whose stories we've told in these pages have, knowingly or not, begun the transformation needed to deliver a Value Experience. They started by keeping the customer first and foremost on the company's mind. For many this change from company-centric to customer-centric vision wasn't easy, as we've seen. It's not comfortable to give up old dictates that tell us business is about sales above all else or to let go of the notion that the company always knows best. But as a Deloitte & Touche study of nine hundred manufacturers showed, customer-centric companies not only have more loyal and satisfied customers, they are 60 percent—60 *percent*—more profitable than companies that turn their eyes inward.[19] That's quite a reward for doing the right thing and putting the customer's needs above your own. For now it's the path less traveled, but we hope that won't be the case for long.

We'd like to end with a list of companies mentioned in this book who have begun their journey on the customer-centric path through one or more components of the Value Experience (table 7-1). They have been priceless teachers and compelling examples of what is possible. When the world of business turns its eyes to the customer, as we think it must, and commits itself to delivering the value people want and deserve, the list will grow. If your name isn't on it yet, we hope it will be soon.

TABLE 7 - 1

Priceless Pioneers

AlpineAire Foods	dcVAST	MSR Mountain
Amazon.com	Dean Foods	National Semiconductor
American Edwards Labs	Deerpath Medical Assoc.	OXO
American Express	DeWALT	Paris Miki
Amtrak	Disney	Pepsi-Cola
Apple Computer	First USA Bank	Pharmacia
BMW	Harley-Davidson	Procter & Gamble
BP	Hewlett-Packard	Pumpkin Masters
Brennan's Restaurant	The Home Depot	Purina Mills
"Bugs" Burger Bug Killers	IBM	Reading Rehabilitation
Buick	Illuminations	Rite Aid
Build-A-Bear Workshop	Intel	Sears
Butterball Turkey	Johnson & Johnson	Sonoco
Caltex Petroleum	Kimberly-Clark	Square D
Campbell Soup Co.	Kroger	Steelcase
Canadian Pacific Hotels	Mario Tricosi	Taco Bell
Circuit City	Marriott Hotels	Tilley Endurables
Cisco Systems	Mercedes-Benz	U.S. Surgical
Cuisinart	Mouton-Rothschild	Xerox

Notes

Beginnings

1. Morris B. Holbrook and Elizabeth C. Hirschman, "The Experiential Aspects of Consumption: Consumer Fantasies, Feelings, and Fun," *Journal of Consumer Research* 9 (1982): 132–140.

2. Joseph B. Pine II and James H. Gilmore, *The Experience Economy: Work Is Theatre & Every Business a Stage* (Boston: Harvard Business School Press, 1999), 12.

3. Pine and Gilmore, *The Experience Economy*, 22.

4. The authors and works that most notably influenced our thinking were: Pine and Gilmore; Bernd H. Schmitt, *Experiential Marketing: How to Get Customers to Sense, Feel, Think, Act, and Relate to Your Company and Brands* (New York: Simon & Schuster, The Free Press, 1999); Morris B. Holbrook, ed., *Consumer Value: A Framework for Analysis and Research* (London: Routledge, 1999); and Holbrook and Hirschman, "The Experiential Aspects of Consumption: Consumer Fantasies, Feelings, and Fun."

5. Deloitte Research, *Making Customer Loyalty Real: Lessons from Leading Manufacturers* (New York: Deloitte & Touche and Deloitte Consulting, 1999), 5.

Chapter 1

1. Morris B. Holbrook, "Introduction to Consumer Value," in *Consumer Value: A Framework for Analysis and Research*, ed. Morris B. Holbrook (London: Routledge, 1999), 1.

2. Ibid.

3. Morris B. Holbrook and Elizabeth C. Hirschman, "The Experiential Aspects of Consumption: Consumer Fantasies, Feelings, and Fun," *Journal of Consumer Research* 9 (1982): 132–140.

4. James C. Anderson and James A. Narus, "Capturing the Value of Supplementary Services," *Harvard Business Review,* January–February 1995, 77.

5. Marsha L. Richins, "Possessions, Materialism, and Other-directedness in the Expression of Self," in *Consumer Value: A Framework for Analysis and Research,* ed. Morris B. Holbrook (London: Routledge, 1999), 85–104.

6. Charles T. Tart, in *Transpersonal Psychologies: Perspectives on the Mind from Seven Great Spiritual Traditions,* 3d ed. [(San Francisco: Harper, 1992), vii–x] describes the whole person as encompassing the body, thought, emotions, and spirit.

7. Abraham Maslow, a renowned psychologist, created the famed "hierarchy of needs." Mihaly Csikszentmihalyi is professor and former chairman of the Department of Psychology at the University of Chicago and author of numerous books and articles on what makes people happy, satisfied, and fulfilled. Morris B. Holbrook is a professor of marketing in the Graduate School of Business at Columbia University and a noted axiologist. Marsha L. Richins is a professor of marketing at the University of Missouri, Columbia, and a researcher on consumers' relationships with their possessions and materialism. Bernd H. Schmitt is a professor at Columbia University's Graduate School of Business in New York and author of *Experiential Marketing: How to Get Customers to Sense, Feel, Think, Act, and Relate to Your Company and Brands.*

8. This is why there was such a strong consumer reaction when Intel shipped a chip with a minor math error that was extremely unlikely to ever occur during typical use. It wasn't the math error that enraged consumers, but what was perceived as a breach of trust by a company that had a reputation for excellence.

9. The Illuminations case study was drawn from the following sources. Authors research and personal experience (Chicago, IL, 2001). California CEO, "CEO Tracker: An Illuminating CEO," *California CEO,* August 2001. Illuminations, "Founder's Letter," <http://www.illuminations.com> (accessed 6 June 2001).

10. Illuminations, "Founder's Letter."

11. Ibid.

12. The BP Connect case study was drawn from the following sources. Author research and personal experience (Chicago, IL 2001). Sara Burnett, "New BP Connect Stores Offer More Conveniences," *The Chicago Daily Herald,* 16 January 2002. Paula Hendrickson, "BP Connect Reinvents the C-Store," *The Journal of Marketing Communications at Retail,* 1 October 2001.

13. Burnett, "New BP Connect Stores Offer More Conveniences."

14. BP is the global corporate brand formed by the combination of British Petroleum, Amoco Corporation, Atlantic Richfield (ARCO), and Burmah Castrol.

15. Hendrickson, "BP Connect Reinvents the C-Store."

16. Ibid.

17. Ibid.

18. Burnett, "New BP Connect Stores Offer More Conveniences."

19. The Gallup Organization, "Environment Not Highest-Priority Issue This Election Year," 2000 Gallup Poll, <http://www.gallup.com/poll/releases> (accessed 25 February 2002).

20. David Lewis and Darren Bridger in their book *The Soul of the New Consumer: Authenticity—What We Buy and Why in the New Economy* [(London: Nicholas Brealey Publishing, 2000), 73–80] present the case that demographics and psychographics are outdated approaches and do not apply to the "new consumer."

21. See article by Marco Vriens and Frankel Ter Hafstede, "Linking Attributes, Benefits, and Consumer Values," *Marketing Research,* 1 October 2000.

22. American Express Press Release, "Too Hooked on Growth? Mid-Sized Companies Turn to Better Expense Control to Improve Margins in Sluggish Economy, American Express Research Finds," American Express, 13 December 2001.

23. Ibid.

24. Ibid.

25. J. Bradford DeLong, "Slouching Towards Utopia? The Economic History of the Twentieth Century," February 1997, <http://econ161.berkely.edu/TCEH/Slouch-roaring 13.html> (accessed 9 May 01).

26. Joseph B. Pine II and James H. Gilmore in their book *Experience Economy: Work Is Theatre & Every Business a Stage* (Boston: Harvard Business School Press, 1999) describe the three shifts in consumer desires as commodities to goods, goods to services, and services to experiences. From a business perspective, these relate to the four economic eras: agrarian, goods, services, and experience.

27. Over the last few years numerous books have been published that discuss the "new consumer." A partial list includes Rolf Jensen, *The Dream Society: How the Coming Shift from Information to Imagination Will Transform Your Business* (New York: McGraw Hill, 1999); Richard W. Oliver, *The Shape of Things to Come: Seven Imperatives for Winning in the New World of Business* (New York: McGraw Hill, 1998); and Lewis and Bridger, *The Soul of the New Consumer.*

Chapter 2

1. Brennan's Restaurant, "History" and "Accolades," see company Web site: <http://www.brennansneworleans.com> (accessed 4 July 2001).

2. Joseph B. Pine II and James H. Gilmore define experience as "events that engage individuals in a personal way" in *Experience Economy: Work Is Theatre & Every Business a Stage* (Boston: Harvard Business School Press, 1999), 3. Bernd H. Schmitt in *Experiential Marketing: How to Get Customers to Sense, Feel, Think, Act, and Relate to Your Company and Brands* [(New York: Simon & Schuster, The Free Press, 1999), 25–26] provides the following description of experiences: "Experiences occur as a result of encountering, undergoing, or living through situations. . . . In sum, experiences provide sensory, emotional, cognitive, behavioral, and relational values that replace functional values."

3. The Amazon.com case study is drawn from author research and personal experience, and Robert Spence, *Amazon.com* (New York: Harper Business, 2002), 29.

4. Spence, *Amazon.com*, 29.

5. Deloitte Research, *Making Customer Loyalty Real: Lessons from Leading Manufacturers* (New York: Deloitte & Touche and Deloitte Consulting, 1999), 20.

6. Ibid.

7. Ibid.

8. Intel Corporation, "Background on the Initial Experience Prediction (IEP) checklist," white paper, 30 April 2001, 2.

9. IBM, "Ease of Use Home," <http://www.ibm.com/ibm/easy> (accessed 1 July 2000).

10. "IBM, Gateway Computer Manufacturers Focus on Sleek, All-in-One Designs," *Miami Herald*, 26 September 2000.

11. Ibid.

12. Ian C. MacMillan and Rita Gunter McGrath, "Discover Your Products' Hidden Potential," *Harvard Business Review*, May–June 1996, 4.

13. Ibid.

14. Sidney Schoeffler, Robert D. Buzzell, and Donald F. Heany, "Impact of Strategic Planning on Profit Performance," *Harvard Business Review*, March–April 1974.

Chapter 3

1. Apple, "Three Steps," Quicktime movie, <http://www.apple.com> (accessed 14 January 2001).

2. The Apple iMac case study was drawn from the following sources. "Apple's iMac a Sales Hit; Firm's Market Share Doubles Thanks to It," *Cincinnati Enquirer*, 22 December 1998. "iMac at Core of Profit," *Electronics Times*, 19 October 1998, 72. Apple, <http://www.apple.com> (accessed 8 February 2001).

3. Johan Arndt, "Reflections on Research in Consumer Behavior," in *Advances in Consumer Research Volume 3*, ed. Beverlee B. Anderson (Ann Arbor, MI: Association for Consumer Research, 1976), 213–221. Arndt identified the five parts of the consumer decision process as recognition, search (for information to evaluate alternatives), purchase, consumption, and post-consumption.

4. Thomas H. Davenport and John C. Beck, *The Attention Economy: Understanding the New Currency of Business* (Boston: Harvard Business School Press, 2001), 4–6.

5. Bernd H. Schmitt, *Experiential Marketing: How to Get Customers to Sense, Feel, Think, Act, and Relate to Your Company and Brands* (New York: Simon & Schuster, The Free Press, 1999), 29.

6. David Lewis and Darren Bridger in their book *The Soul of the New Consumer: Authenticity—What We Buy and Why in the New Economy* [(London: Nicholas Brealey Publishing, 2000), 9] provide this description of the new consumers' scarcity of attention: "Unless they are able to understand something quickly and easily it will often be ignored, especially when the personal relevance of the information is unclear."

7. RCA Advertisement, *Newsweek*, 3 December 2001, 67.

8. The Great Indoors, Web site, <http://www.thegreatindoors.com> (accessed 4 February 2002).

9. David Kenny and John F. Marshall, "Contextual Marketing: The Real Business of the Internet," *Harvard Business Review,* November–December 2000, 122.

10. Lewis and Bridger, *Soul of the New Consumer.*

11. Davenport and Beck, *The Attention Economy,* 1–15.

12. Already 16 percent of car buyers go online before showing up at a dealership (Gary Hamel and Jeff Sampler, "The E-Corporation," *Fortune,* 7 December 1998). According to an ACNielsen survey, the top four uses of the Internet are, respectively: e-mail, general surfing, to gather information on a product or service, and to purchase a product or service (Grace Hyatt, "The Internet Shopper: A Closer Look," *Consumer Insight,* June 2000, 6). Lewis and Bridger, *Soul of the New Consumer,* 18.

13. The Rogaine case study was drawn from author research and personal experience (Chicago, IL, 2001). Kellie Hale, telephone conversation with authors, 12 November 2001.

14. In response to the impact of the Internet on consumers, Richard Oliver in the book *The Shape of Things to Come* [(London: McGraw-Hill, 1999), 57] wrote the following: "The day of the passive consumer has vanished. If not willingly provided with the full information they want, customers go elsewhere with little hesitation."

15. Terry Britton, Cisco partner facility tour (Chicago, IL, May 2000).

16. Associated Press, "Self-Serve Checkouts a Hit with Managers, Shoppers," *Greensboro News & Record,* 7 August 1999.

17. Don Swanson, interview by authors, Chicago, IL, 15 December 2001.

18. Ibid.

19. Ibid.

20. Cliff Edwards, "Dean Milking Big Sales from Chugs Grab-and-Go Drinks Are a Hit with Consumers," *Peoria Journal Star,* 24 August 1998.

21. Ibid.

22. Ibid.

23. Patricia Siebel, "Customer Satisfaction: The Fundamental Basis of Business Survival," white paper, February 2001, 6–7.

24. Ibid.

25. Marc Gobé in his book *Emotional Branding: The New Paradigm for Connecting Brands to People* (New York: Allworth Press, 2001) presents the case that brands must connect with consumers on a personal and holistic level on the issues that are most important to them. He describes the new business model as "one of brands connecting with innovative products that are culturally relevant, socially sensitive, and have presence at all points of contact in people's lives."

26. Schmitt, *Experiential Marketing,* 29.

27. Campbell Soup Press Release, "Second-Grader Creates New Verse to Classic M'm! M'm! Good! Jingle Campbell's Labels For Education™ Rewards Student's School with Music Equipment" (North Salem, IN: 24 April, 2001).

28. Jeff Bedard, e-mail to authors, 27 March 2002.

29. Steelcase Web site: <http://www.steelcase.com/knowledgebase/faqs.htm> (accessed 5 July 2001).

30. The Purina Mills case study was drawn from the following sources. Diana LaSalle Deterding, consulting engagement with Purina Mills (Chicago, IL, 1997). Ronni

Sayewitz, "Purina Targets 'Ruralpolitan' Niche With New Retail Stores," *Dallas Business Journal*, 24 July 1998, 3.

31. Deloitte Research, *Making Customer Loyalty Real: Lessons from Leading Manufacturers* (New York: Deloitte & Touche and Deloitte Consulting, 1999), 5.

Part 2 Opener

1. The Build-A-Bear Workshop case study was drawn from author research and personal experiences (Chicago, IL, May 2001); and Cheryl Hall, "The Right Stuff," *The Dallas Morning News,* 22 October 2000. Build-A-Bear Workshop, "About Us," <http://www.buildabear.com> (accessed 12 December 2000).

2. Hall, "The Right Stuff."

3. Ibid.

4. The average annual sales per square foot for toy and hobby stores in 1999 were $310. Dougal M. Casey and Michael Baker, ed., *A 1999 U.S. Retail Sales, Mall Sales, and Department Store Sales Review* (International Council of Shopping Centers, 2000).

Chapter 4

1. The OXO case study was drawn from the following sources. Author research and personal experience (Chicago, IL, 2001). Bruce Nussbaum, "How Great Products Can Boost the Bottom Line," *BusinessWeek,* November 1999. Corporate Design Foundation, "Getting a Grip on Kitchen Tools," *@issue* 2, no. 1. OXO International, "Swivel Peeler Case Study," <http://www.oxo.com> (accessed 19 August 2001).

2. Deloitte Research describes the relationship between product design and experience in a white paper titled *Creating Unique Customer Experiences: The Next Stage of Integrated Product Development* (New York: Deloitte & Touche and Deloitte Consulting, 2000), "New product development in the manufacturing industry is undergoing a radical change. 'Eureka'—or a great idea—is not enough to beat the competition. To gain customer loyalty, manufacturing organizations must design new products that create value-added 'experiences' tailored to each customer."

3. OXO International, "Swivel Peeler Case Study."

4. Nussbaum, "How Great Products Can Boost the Bottom Line."

5. Ibid.

6. The Amtrak Coast Starlight case study was drawn from the following sources. Lora J. Finnegan, "A New Coast Starlight Rolls Out," *Sunset Magazine,* October 1996, 28. Amtrak, "Coast Starlight," <http://www.amtrak.com/trains/coaststarlight.html> (accessed 16 November 2001). Business Wire Press Release, "Amtrak Launches New 'Pacific Surfliner' Passenger Rail Service" (Oakland, CA: Business Wire, June 2000). Amtrak, "Amtrak Travel Planner: What A Difference The Train Makes," 2001.

7. Amtrak, "Coast Starlight," <http://www.amtrak.com/trains/coaststarlight.html> (accessed 16 November 2001).

8. According to Paco Underhill, author of *Why We Buy: The Science of Shopping* [(New York: Simon & Schuster, 1999), 161–162], ". . . virtually all unplanned purchases— and many planned ones, too—come as a result of the shopper seeing, touching, smelling or tasting something that promises pleasure, if not total fulfillment."

9. Donald A. Norman in his book *The Design of Everyday Things* (New York: Doubleday, 1990), 4, states that, "... one of the most important principles of design [is]: *visibility.*"

10. According to Paco Underhill in *Why We Buy,* 162, "We buy things today more than ever based on trial and touch."

11. Corporate Design Foundation, "Getting a Grip on Kitchen Tools."

12. Scott Miller, "Why BMW Obsesses Over Every Whir and Thunk—Acoustics Are the New Frontier in Designing Luxury Cars; A Little Brahms, Anyone?" *Wall Street Journal,* 14 January 2002. Reprinted by permission of *Wall Street Journal,* Copyright © 2002 Dow Jones & Company, Inc. All Rights Reserved Worldwide. License number 507771233642.

13. Ibid.

14. Ibid.

15. David Lewis and Darren Bridger in their book *The Soul of the New Consumer: Authenticity—What We Buy and Why in the New Economy* [(London: Nicholas Brealey Publishing, 2000), 33] state that, "It is, in large part, a brand's ability to trigger certain such emotional responses that provides it with a winning edge over less familiar products and services."

16. Buick, "The Best in PGA Tour Action," <http://www.buick.com/golf> (accessed 13 January 2002).

Chapter 5

1. Schneider Electric, "Square D/Schneider Electric: A Click-and-Mortar Company Leads the Web Way," *PR Newswire,* Palatine, IL, 17 July 2000.

2. University of Michigan, "American Customer Satisfaction Plateaus for Second Quarter 2001," Customer Care Institute Web site, <http://www.customercare.com/industry_news> (accessed 17 November 2001).

3. Frederick F. Reichheld, *The Loyalty Effect: The Hidden Force Behind Growth, Profits, and Lasting Value* (Boston: Harvard Business School Press, 1996), 36.

4. Deloitte Research, *Making Customer Loyalty Real: Lessons from Leading Manufacturers* (New York: Deloitte & Touche and Deloitte Consulting, 1999), 22–32.

5. Alan W. H. Grant and Leonard A. Schlesinger, "Realize Your Customer's Full Profit Potential," *Harvard Business Review,* September–October 1995, 69.

6. Julie M. Hays and Arthur V. Hill, "Gaining Competitive Service Value Through Performance Motivation," *Journal of Strategic Performance Measurement,* October/November 1999, 36–40. M. Hocutt and T. Stone, "The Impact of Employee Empowerment on the Quality of Service Recovery Effort," *Journal of Quality Management* 3, no. 1 (1998).

7. Richard B. Chase and Sriram Dasu, "Want to Perfect Your Company's Service? Use Behavioral Science," *Harvard Business Review,* June 2001, 80.

8. Ibid.

9. Richard J. Schuster and Marianne L. Weber, "Quantitative Methods in Healthcare: Contributing to Customer Satisfaction and Quality Design," *The Academy Journal* 2, part 1, October 1999.

10. Jody Hoffer Gittell and Mason Brown, "Reading Rehabilitation Hospital: Implementing Patient-Focused Care," Case 9-898-172 (Boston: Harvard Business School, 2000).

11. For additional information see the article by Youngme Moon and Frances X. Frei, "Exploding the Self-Service Myth," *Harvard Business Review,* May–June 2000.

12. Denise Duclaux, "Dare to Be Different," *ABA Banking Journal,* September 1995, 65.

13. R. T. Mills and D. S. Krantz, "Information, Choice, and Reactions to Stress: A Field Experiment in a Blood Bank with Laboratory Analogue," *Journal of Personality and Social Psychology* 37 (1979): 608–620.

14. Chase and Dasu, "Want to Perfect Your Company's Service? " 83.

15. Christopher Selenta, Brenda E. Hogan, and Wolfgang Linden, "How Often Do Office Blood Pressure Measurements Fail to Identify True Hypertension?" *Archives of Family Medicine* 9, no. 6 (2000): 533–540.

16. Christopher W. L. Hart, "The Power of Unconditional Service Guarantees," *Harvard Business Review,* July–August 1988, 54–62.

17. Ibid.

18. Chase and Dasu, "Want to Perfect Your Company's Service?" 84.

19. Hart, "The Power of Unconditional Service Guarantees."

20. The National Semiconductor case study was drawn from the following sources. Transim Press Release, "National Semiconductor Introduces POWER.NATIONAL .COM," <http://www.transim.com> (accessed 11 Aug 2001). Patricia B. Seybold, "Get Inside the Lives of Your Customers," *Harvard Business Review,* May 2001, 81–89. National Semiconductor Press Release, "National Semiconductor Wins 'Outstanding Web Site' Award for Corporate Web Site Excellence" (Santa Clara, CA: National Semiconductor, 8 December 1998). Author research and personal experience (Chicago, IL, March 2001).

21. Transim Press Release, "National Semiconductor Introduces POWER. NATIONAL.COM," <http://www.transim.com> (accessed 11 Aug 2001).

22. Seybold, "Get Inside the Lives of Your Customers."

23. The Paris Miki case study is drawn from the following sources. Paris Miki, "Paris-Miki Optical Uses Modern Computer Technology to Design Thoroughly Individual Glasses," <http:www.paris-miki.com.au/cgmachine.htm> (accessed 11 August 2001). Eric Torbenson, "Mass Customization: As You Like It," *CIO Enterprise Magazine,* 15 February 1998.

24. Dana James, "Lighting the Way," *Marketing News,* 1 April 2002, 1, 11. Reprinted with permission from *Marketing News,* published by the American Marketing Association, Dana James, 1 April 2002, 1, 11.

Chapter 6

1. William J. Dowlding, *Beatlesongs* (New York: Fireside, 1989), 220. Judson Knight, *Abby Road to Zapple Records: A Beatles Encyclopedia* (Dallas, TX: Taylor Publishing Company, 1997), 27–29.

2. According to Paco Underhill in his book *Why We Buy: The Science of Shopping* [(New York: Simon & Schuster, 1999), 81] "Another obvious place to look for experiential executions is in packaging. Indeed, consumers have become increasingly attentive to packaging and have higher and higher expectations of it."

3. Packaging can also play a unique role in portraying your products' aesthetic attributes during the evaluate stage. Paco Underhill provides several examples of packaging design that uses touch, sight, and smell to promote the product in his book *Why We Buy*.

4. The Pepsi-Cola case study is drawn from Ian C. MacMillan and Rita Gunther McGrath, "Discover Your Product's Hidden Potential," *Harvard Business Review*, May–June 1996; and Steven Truitt, "The History Of Pepsi-Cola," <http://www.angelfire.com/ga/struitt/pepsi.html> (accessed 26 August 2001).

5. Bret Carlson, "Use It. Return It," *Assembly*, September 1999.

6. Ric Deterding, telephone conversation with authors, 24 February 2001.

7. Hallie Forcinio, "10 Turning Points in Pharmaceutical Packaging," *Pharmaceutical Technology* 25, no. 7 (2001): 115.

8. Thomas Matthews, "A Love Affair of Art and Life," *Wine Spectator*, 31 May 1995.

9. The Mouton-Rothschild case study is drawn from Matthews, "A Love Affair of Art and Life"; Mouton-Rothschild, "Guided Tour," <http://www.bpdr.com> (accessed 7 April 2001); and Gian Luigi Longinotti-Buitoni, *Selling Dreams: How to Make Any Product Irresistible* (New York: Simon & Schuster, 1999), 140–142.

10. Studies conducted by Envirosell showed that 91 percent of customers buy skin-care products only after reading the front label, and 42 percent also read the back of the package. Underhill, *Why We Buy*, 131.

11. Underhill states that, "Amenability (of the shopping environment) and profitability are totally and inextricably linked. Take care of the former, in all its guises, and the latter is assured" (*Why We Buy*, 44).

12. A study conducted by David Lewis and Darren Bridger and cited in their book *The Soul of the New Consumer: Authenticity—What We Buy and Why in the New Economy* [(London: Nicholas Brealey Publishing, 2000), 128–147] showed that shopper stress can sometimes rise as high as that of a policeman confronting a rioting mob or combat pilots flying into action. According to the authors, their research suggests that four main factors contribute to shopper stress: congestion, time delays, difficulties in locating required items, and intrusive atmosphere. They also name several minor factors, including poor signage, narrow and congested aisles, and checkout queues.

13. Richard Bierck, "Are You Reaching Your Customers?" *Harvard Management Communication Letter*, December 2000, 3.

14. Roy S. Johnson, "Home Depot Renovates," <http://www.fortune.com> (accessed 4 March 2001).

15. Larry Shalzi, telephone conversation with authors, 10 March 2001.

16. Johnson, "Home Depot Renovates."

17. Bierck, "Are You Reaching Your Customers?"

18. Joyce Hanson, "It's a Brave New World in Retail-Store Designs," *Central Penn Business Journal*, 21 August 1998.

19. Ibid.

20. The Rite Aid case study is drawn from Hanson, "It's a Brave New World in Retail-Store Designs"; Rite Aid, *Year 2000 Annual Report*, 1–2; and Rite Aid Press Release, "Rite Aid Announces First Quarter Results; Achieves EBITDA of $165.0 Million," Rite Aid, Camp Hill, PA, 11 July 2001.

21. Survey conducted by authors, 21 May 2001.

22. Terry Britton, employee of American Edwards Labs (Irvine, CA, 1982).

Chapter 7

1. Karl Albrecht and Ron Zemke, *Service America: Doing Business in the New Economy* (Warner Books, 1995), 13.

2. Dorothy Leonard and Jeffrey F. Rayport, "Spark Innovation Through Emphatic Design," *Harvard Business Review,* November–December 1997, 104.

3. Alan W. H. Grant and Leonard A. Schlesinger, "Realize Your Customers' Full Profit Potential," *Harvard Business Review,* September–October 1995, 65.

4. Grant and Schlesinger, "Realize Your Customers' Full Profit Potential," 62.

5. Grant and Schlesinger, 65.

6. Diana LaSalle Deterding, Horse Industry Alliance Board of Directors (Lexington, KY, 1997–1998).

7. Ibid.

8. The Mercedes AAV story is drawn from Olive Keogh, "Mercedes Aims at Young Drivers with M-class," *Automotive News Europe,* 3 March 1998; Mercedes Benz, "Life Is in Season All the Year Round," M-Class Overview, <http://www.mercedes-benz.co.za/pc/classes/M/default.htm> (accessed 12 November 2001); Skip Wollenberg, "Ed Sullivan Appears in Ads for New Mercedes Sports Utility Vehicle," *Consumer News,* 8 September 1997; and Daimler-Chrysler press release, 22 January 2001.

9. Keogh, "Mercedes Aims at Young Drivers with M-class."

10. Mercedes Benz, "Life Is in Season All the Year Round."

11. Wollenberg, "Ed Sullivan Appears in Ads for New Mercedes Sports Utility Vehicle."

12. Thomas A. Stewart, "The Leading Edge: A Satisfied Customer Isn't Enough," *Fortune Magazine,* 21 July 1997.

13. Ibid.

14. Leonard and Rayport, "Spark Innovation Through Emphatic Design," 107.

15. Leonard and Rayport, 104.

16. Leonard and Rayport, 105.

17. Leonard and Rayport, 107.

18. Jim Billington, "Customer-Driven Innovation," *Harvard Management Update,* July 1998.

19. Deloitte Research, *Making Customer Loyalty Real: Lessons from Leading Manufacturers* (New York: Deloitte & Touche and Deloitte Consulting, 1999), 1.

Index

accessibility, 57, 136–139
  Internet, 141–142
acquire stage, 56–61, 68. *See also*
  Experience Engagement Process
  choice in, 59–61
  environment and, 122
  rewards in, 58–59
  sacrifices in, 57–58, 61
advertising
  consumer savvy about, 52–53
  discover stage and, 49–50
  Mercedes M-Class, 153–154
  retail locations in, 52
aesthetic attributes, 78–79, 88–95
  sight, 89–90
  smell, 94–95
  sound, 92–94
  taste, 95
  touch, 90–92
affordability, 106–107
airline call centers, 102–104
AlpineAire Foods, 126–127
Amazon.com, 31–33
AMD, 12–13

American Edwards Labs, 138–139
American Express, 21–23
  @ Work, 22–23
America's Country Store, 67–68
Amtrak, 87–88
Apple Computers
  iMac, 47–48, 50, 84
associative attributes, 79, 96–97
atmosphere, 131–135
  on the Web, 139–140
automobile sound engineering, 92–93
availability, 7
axiology, 6–7

Bananas Foster, 27–28
Bed, Bath & Beyond, 57, 137
benefits versus experiences, 82
BMW, 92–93
BP Connect, 16–18
Brennan's Restaurant, 27–28
"Bugs" Burger Bug Killers, 112–113
Buick, 96–97
Build-A-Bear Workshop, 71–74

business models, 24–25
business revolutions, 24–25
Business Week, 84

Calphalon, 97
Caltex Petroleum, 42–43
Campbell Soup Company, 65–66
Canadian Pacific Hotels, 154–156
caring, 102, 117–119
Caterpillar, 97
CD-ROMs, 42
child-resistant caps, 122, 127
choice, 59–61
Circuit City, 142
Cisco Systems, 55–56
Coast Starlight, 87–88
Coca-Cola, 124
commoditization, 15–18
  definition of, 15
community, 55
company-induced consumption, 49–50
compartmentalization, 103–104
component manufacturing, 55–56
computers
  iMacs, 47–48, 50, 84
  setting up new, 36–37, 61–62
consistency, 106–108
consumers. *See also* service
  acting as your own, 64
  complexity of modern, 65–68
  determining values of, 18–23
  environmentalism and, 17
  environment input from, 138–139
  evolution of, 23–26
  identifying wants of, 12–14
  information evaluation by, 53–56
  information gathering about, 145–162
  insights from, 156–162
  interaction of with products, 28, 29, 72–73
  partnerships with, 66–67
  personalizing experience for, 31–33

rewards and sacrifices of, 38–45
roles of, 24–25
consumption
  discover stage and, 49–53
  experiential view of, xiii–xiv
  integrate stage in, 61–64
  motivation in, 3
  sight in, 89–90
  value as basis for, 6
context, 33–34
control, 60
Copco, 77. *See also* OXO Good Grips
cost, 7–8
cost-in-use studies, 8
credit cards
  affinity, 147–148
  corporate, 21–23
cruise lines, 107–108
Cuisinart hand blender, 82–84
culture, service and, 117–119
cumulative value, 12–14
customer-centric view, 74–75, 161–162
customer satisfaction, 100.
  See also service
customization
  Amazon.com and, 31–33

DaimlerChrysler, 151
dcVAST, 59–60, 88
Dean Foods, 62–63
decision-making models, 49
Deerpath Medical Associates, 44–45
Deloitte & Touche, 161
design
  in product development, 80–84
  profit and, 84
Designs of the Decade: Best in Business
  1990–1999 Awards, 84
DeWALT drills, 91–92, 97
differentiation
  commoditization and, 15–18
  packaging as, 125

discover stage, 49–53. *See also* Experience
    Engagement Process
    enabling value evaluation in, 50–51
dispatch centers, 85–86

economic conditions, 20–23
education, consumer, 67–68
efficiency, 7–8, 106–107
emotional level, 9, 65
    in value model, 12–13
employees
    empowering, 103–104
    service culture and, 117–119
empowerment, 103–105, 118
    labels and, 129–130
environment, 74, 75, 121–143
    customer input on, 138–139
    definition of, 122
    macro-, 122, 131–139
    micro-, 122, 123–131
    packaging and, 122
    retail spaces, 122
environmental issues, 17
evaluate stage, 53–56, 68. *See also*
    Experience Engagement Process
    try before you buy in, 55–56
evolution, 23–26
expectations, 106–108
experience, 27–45
    context and, 33–34
    definition of, 3, 28, 29–30
    desire for, 2–3
    determining overall impact of, 39–41
    engineering improvement in, 115–116
    events, 29, 34–37
    holistic nature of, 82
    individual on a mass scale, 26
    interactions in, 28, 29, 72–73
    managing, 47–69
    reactions in, 28, 29–30
    rewards and sacrifices in, 38–45
    sequence of events in, 107–108

unique nature of, 30–33
value and, xiii–xv, 1–3, 37–38
Experience Economy, The (Pine,
    Gilmore), xiii
Experience Engagement Process, 3,
    47–69
    acquire stage in, 56–61
    analysis of, 161
    discover stage in, 49–53
    evaluate stage in, 53–56
    extend stage in, 65–68
    integrate stage in, 61–64
    service and, 118–119
    value of, 97
experience event matrixes, 39–41
experiential view, xiii
extend stage, 65–68. *See also* Experience
    Engagement Process
    microenvironment and, 130–131

facilitation, extension through, 67–68
FACT concept, 149
Farber, Sam, 77–78, 80
features
    versus experiences, 82
    withholding, 91–92
Federal Express, 104–105
Fix Me service, 110–114
    guarantees in, 112–113
    pain management in, 110–111
    pain prevention in, 111–114
    remedies in, 113–114
freeze-dried foods, 126–127
Furniture Management Coalition, 67

Give Me More service, 114–119
    group, 114–116
    individualized, 116–119
Great Indoors, 51–52, 56
grocery stores
    Kroger, 58–59, 60

grocery stores (*continued*)
  purchase tracking in, 147
guarantees of service, 112–113, 119

health care, 44–45
  blood pressure checks and, 111–112
  hospitals and, 108–109
Help Me service, 101–105
  airline call centers and, 102–104
  Federal Express and, 104–105
Hewlett-Packard, 93, 157
Holter monitors, 138–139
Home Depot, The, 94–95, 132–133
  Web site of, 139–140
Horse Industry Alliance, 150–151
hospitals, 108–109. *See also* health care

IBM
  Ease of Use organization, 36–37
  NetVista X40, 37
  PC setup and, 36–37
Illuminations, 14–15
iMacs, 47–48, 50, 84
Industrial Revolution, 25
information
  consumer evaluation of, 53–56
  consumer insights, 156–162
  about customers, 145–162
  gathering, 161
  historical data, 146–149
  labels and, 129–130
  understanding, 150–156
Information Age, 53
informed observers, 158–159
innovation, 156–162
insight, 156–162
integrate stage, 61–64, 68. *See also*
    Experience Engagement Process
  environment and, 122
  Internet value in, 140–141
  services and, 63–64

intellectual level, 9
  in value model, 12–13
Internet. *See also* Web sites
  accessibility on, 141–142
  atmosphere on, 139–140
  organization on, 140–141
  shopping convenience via, 60

Johnson & Johnson, 52
Journal of Consumer Research, xiii

key words, 141
Kimberly-Clark, 160
Kroger, 58–59, 60

labels, 65–66, 128–131
  information in, 129–130
Labels for Education program, 65–66
laddering, 19
loyalty, 65–66, 161
  customer service and, 101
Loyalty Effect, The (Reichheld), 101

macroenvironment, 122, 131–139, 143
  accessibility in, 136–139
  atmosphere in, 122–135
  Internet as, 139–142
  organization and, 135–136
mail-order returns, 130
Mario Tricosi Hair Salon and Day Spas,
    133–134
marketing
  associative attributes and, 96–97
  discover stage and, 49–50
market research, 18–19, 138–139,
    145–162. *See also* consumers; Value
    Groups
Marriott International, 63–64
MasterCard, 147–148

McDonald's, 105, 106–107
Mercedes-Benz
    All Activity Vehicle, 151–154
    sound engineering of, 92
    visual attributes of, 90
metatags, 141
microenvironment, 122, 123–131, 142
    failures in, 126–127
    labeling and, 128–131
    packaging, 123–127
microevolution, 24
milk, 62–63
Milk Chug, 62–63
Miller/Zell, 137–138
morale, employee, 103–104
motivation, in consumption, 3
Mouton-Rothschild wines, 128–129
MSR Mountain, 127

National Semiconductor, 115–116
NetVista X40, 37
neutral events, 39–40, 84
Nissan Design International, 147, 158–159

objective value, 7–8, 11
O'Hare International Airport, 133
opportunities, identifying, 34–37
optical chains, 116–117
organization, 135–136
    on the Web, 140–141
out-of-box experience (OOBE), 36–37
OXO Good Grips, 77–78, 84
    accessibility of, 57, 137
    physical attributes of, 80–82
    touch aesthetic of, 91

packaging, 121, 123–127
    differentiation through, 125
    factors to consider in, 127
    of milk, 62–63

returnable containers, 125–126
pain management, 110–111
Paris Miki, 116–117
partnerships with consumers, 66–67
Pentium chips, 12–13
Pepsi-Cola, 124–125
perceptions, value and, 12–14
personalization, 57
    on the Internet, 142
Pharmacia, 53–55, 67
physical attributes, 78, 79–84
    of Cuisinart hand blender, 82–84
    of OXO Good Grips Peeler, 80–82
    as sacrifices, 84
physical level, 9
    in value model, 12–13
Pringles, 130
process attributes, 78, 85–88
    of Coast Starlight, 87–88
    Give Me More service and, 114–119
    individualized service and, 116–117
Procter & Gamble, 145–146
product, 74, 77–98
    aesthetic attributes of, 78–79, 88–95
    associative attributes of, 79, 96–97
    physical attributes of, 78, 79–84
    process attributes of, 78, 85–88
    roles of, 78
    services as, 85–88
product development, 80–82
profitability drivers, 24–25
profit margins, 20–23
profits
    design and, 84
    loyalty and, 101, 161
Purina Mills, 67–68

quantity, 11

radio, 158
RCA Scenium HDTVs, 50–51

Reading Rehabilitation hospital,
108–109
remedies, service, 113–114
repair service, 110–114
response times, 111
retail spaces, 122. *See also* environment
accessibility in, 136–139
atmosphere in, 131–135
returnable containers, 125–126
rewards, 3, 38–45
acquire stage, 58–59
environment and, 133–134
identifying impact of, 40
product attributes and, 97
turning sacrifices into, 42–43
Rite Aid, 117–119, 135–136
Rogaine, 53–55, 67
Rothschild, Philippe de, 128
routine, 105–106

sacrifices, 3, 38–45
acquire stage and, 57–58, 61
environment and, 133–134
identifying impact of, 40
negative physical attributes and, 84
product attributes and, 97
self-serve as, 108–109
turning into rewards, 42–43
Santoprene, 80, 91
Schneider Electric, 100
search engines, 141
Sears
Craftsman Low Profile Wet/Dry
Vacuum, 159–160
Great Indoors, 51–52, 56
seating, 133–134
self-induced consumption, 49, 51–52
self-serve, 108–109
semiconductor design, 115–116
Serve Me service, 105–109
expectations and, 106–108
the whole process in, 108–109
service, 74

culture of, 117–119
Fix Me, 110–114
Give Me More, 114–119
goal of, 100
guarantees, 112–113, 119
Help Me, 101–105
importance of, 100
remedies in, 113–114
routine in, 105–108
self-serve, 108–109
Serve Me, 105–109
service contracts, 59–60
service era, 25–26
service industries
atmosphere and, 133–134
compared with manufacturing, 85
integrate stage and, 63–64
process attributes in, 85–88
shelter, 13–14
shop vacuums, 159–160
sight, 89–90
situation-induced consumption, 49, 52
Smart Design, 77, 80
smell, 94–95
Sonoco Product Company
Industrial Containers Division, 7–8
Soul of the New Consumer (Lewis,
Bridger), 52
sound, 92–94
spiritual level, 9–10, 65
in value model, 12–13
sports utility vehicles, 151–154
SQAD, 16
Square D, 99–100
Steelcase, 66–67
Stowell, Davin, 77–78, 91
structured interviews, 19
subjective value, 7, 8, 10–12
System Link universal remote, 90

Taco Bell, 148–150
taste, sense of, 95
Thomson Consumer Electronics, 90

Tilley Endurables Hats, 1–3, 112
touch, 90–92

United States Surgical Corporation
  (U.S. Surgical), 34–35
Universal Design, 77–78

value, 5–25
  commoditization and, 15–18
  criteria for assigning, 7–8
  cumulative, 12–14
  discover stage and, 50–51
  evolution of, 23–26
  experience and, xiii–xv, 1–3
  with Give Me More service, 114–119
  nature of, 6–8
  objective and subjective, 7–8, 11
  rewards and sacrifices in, 38–45
  whole person and, 9–11
Value Experiences, 37–38, 42–43
  components of, 74
  determining desired, 88
  environment in, 74, 121–143
  in health care, 44–45
  importance of, 43
  product in, 74, 77–98
  service in, 74, 99–119
  statements of, 153–154
Value Groups, 6, 18–23
  definition of, 18
  identifying, 161
  Mercedes-Benz, 152–153
  service and, 118–119

  service levels and, 88
  Taco Bell, 148–150
Value Model, 11–18, 161
values
  associative attributes and, 96–97
  determining consumer, 18–23,
   151–158
  evolution of, 23–26
  in experiences, 30–33
  extend stage and, 65–68
Visa, 147–148
visual experiences, 89–90

Wacker Chemical Corporation, 21–23
wait periods, 133, 134
Walt Disney Company, 42
Webench, 115–116
Web sites
  accessibility and, 141–142
  atmosphere in, 139–140
  butterball.com, 140
  Circuit City, 142
  Home Depot, The, 139–140
  Illuminations, 15
  organization in, 140–141
  Pharmacia (Rogaine), 54–55, 67
  Webench, 115–116
"White Album" (Beatles), 121
whole person, value and, 9–11
Wine Spectator, 129
Wurlitzer jukeboxes, 89

Xerox, 111

About the Authors

TERRY A. BRITTON has more than twenty years of experience identifying customer needs and delivering customer-centric solutions in service industries. For eleven years he was the chief technical officer at dcVAST, Inc., an IT services and consulting company near Chicago, Illinois. A partner for nearly a decade, he was instrumental in helping the business sustain a 37 percent annual growth rate, posting above-average profits for each year of the company's life. Prior to this position, he was with Baxter International, where he served as national service manager, manager of business development, and director of operations.

Throughout his career Terry has been recognized as a forward thinker, speaking on business vision and new technologies at seminars and events sponsored by Sun Microsystems, Intel, Hewlett-Packard, and other industry leaders. He has written several white papers and business and technical briefs, including *Network-Centric Computing in the 21st Century*.

DIANA LASALLE has spent more than two decades helping businesses understand the customer. For eighteen years she was the principal of Dymar Agency, a Chicago-based advertising firm specializing in niche and affinity markets. She has worked with a diverse range of clients, including Purina Mills, the Smithsonian Institution's National Museum of Natural History, Pfizer, Bayer, the American Quarter Horse Association, and Wrangler, to create education and experience programs and strategies.

In addition to her consulting work, Diana is a sought-after speaker and has given seminars and workshops on value and the customer's role in experience. She has also published over a dozen articles on business and marketing strategy in trade and professional journals.

Diana and Terry are the principals of True North Strategies of Savannah, Georgia. The firm is dedicated to helping businesses understand and improve the customer experience and develop a comprehensive view of the value they can offer.

More from *Priceless*

Would you like to know what an OXO Good Grips peeler looks like or what a child sees when she walks into a Build-a-Bear Workshop? Do you want to know more about the companies featured in *Priceless* or read up on the latest *Priceless* case studies? Then visit *www.Pricelessthebook.com*. There you'll find photos, links, and stories, including background research that didn't make the final manuscript. We've also assembled the Priceless Roadmap suggestions into a single PDF file for easy reference.

For those of you who would like to share your customer experience successes or suggestions, the Web site also includes a feedback section, as well as a way to contact us for questions or comments.